Getting Published

This guide for new and practising lecturers and researchers takes a rare insider's look at the activities of writing and publishing. Turning the spotlight inwards, it examines how and why professionals communicate with each other through writing and publishing.

Written with great verve and pace, the author provides sensible advice bolstered by his own research, using many illustrative examples, case studies, and anecdotes. For the academic needing insight into the serious business of getting published, this book will provide answers to many of their frequent questions:

- Why do people write and publish, and who are they writing for?
- What channels of communication are available for their writing, and who 'controls' them?
- How can they successfully submit articles and papers to journals and newspapers, contribute chapters to books, or approach publishers with book proposals?

Developed from a series of seminars and new empirical research on the subject by the author, this book will be an enjoyable and informative guide to anyone determined to see their name in print.

Jerry Wellington is Professor in the School of Education, University of Sheffield.

Getting Published

A guide for lecturers and researchers

Jerry Wellington

RoutledgeFalmer
Taylor & Francis Group

LONDON AND NEW YORK

First published 2003
by RoutledgeFalmer
11 New Fetter Lane, London EC4P 4EE

Simultaneously published in the USA and Canada
by RoutledgeFalmer
29 West 35th Street, New York, NY 10001

RoutledgeFalmer is an imprint of the Taylor & Francis Group

© 2003 Jerry Wellington

Typeset in Goudy and Gill by BC Typesetting, Bristol
Printed and bound in Great Britain by
TJ International Ltd, Padstow, Cornwall

British Library Cataloguing in Publication Data
A catalogue record for this book is available from the British Library

Library of Congress Cataloging in Publication Data
Wellington, J. J. (Jerry J.)
  Getting published: a guide for lecturers and researchers/Jerry Wellington.
    p.   cm. – (Routledge study guides)
  Includes bibliographical references and index.
  1. Authorship–Marketing. 2. Scholarly publishing. I. Title. II. Series.

PN161.W37 2003
070.52–dc21   2003046554

ISBN 0–415–29847–4

Contents

Preface

This book is an attempt to look inside the activities of writing and publishing. My objective is to turn the spotlight inwards and examine how groups of professionals communicate with each other, and with outsiders in some cases, by writing and publishing. Why do they write and publish? Who are they writing for? What channels of communication are available for their writing? Who 'controls' these channels? Is the peer-review process an aid to writers or a barrier? What guidance and advice can be offered to those who wish to 'get published'? How can writers acquire that imprimatur, the official licence to print?

Nobody publishes without writing, but people often write without publishing – here we focus on publishing (whatever the outlet) as an end product of writing. The book is aimed at anyone with an interest in getting work published, in continuing to publish or in the publishing process in general. Examples, and my own experiences, are drawn from the field of education – but much of the literature discussed comes from other areas (the sciences, the social sciences and the humanities). In addition, data are drawn from seminars, discussion groups, interviews with writers and journal editors, and answers to my questions from the major book publishers in the UK.

To my knowledge, the title 'Getting Published' was first used in an article in the 1970s (Mahoney et al., 1978). It was used nineteen years later in a fascinating ESRC research project conducted by Angela Packwood, Margaret Scanlon and Gaby Weiner (Packwood et al., 1997). Their study explored the whole business of getting published at that time: peer review, editing, writing, the content of journals, and contributors to journals. That project was one of the stimuli for this one.

I would like to acknowledge the help of all the people who gave their time up in interviews, discussion groups and seminars or by writing helpful e-mails in response to my questions. I agreed not to name any of my 'informants', but they may recognize their voices and their contributions if they read this book. I would like to single out two Ph.D. students, Gill Bielby and Mark Vickers, and four colleagues, Cheryl Hunt, Elaine Millard, Maria Mawson and Tom Wilson, to thank them for their time in discussing some of the ideas and in reading early drafts of the chapters and giving valuable feedback.

In a nutshell, this book looks inside the writing process that is sometimes treated as a secret garden. It looks inside the can of worms that is the editorial process. It explores beneath the tip of the iceberg of peer review and the black box that emits the dreaded referees' comments. The book also counsels against using and mixing tired, worn-out metaphors. I hope that readers find the book interesting and useful. If you have any constructive criticisms, praise or pleasant comments, please tell me at j.wellington@sheffield.ac.uk. If you have any scathing remarks, please send them to the publishers.

Chapter 1

Why publish?

A whole host of reasons is given in answering this question. Some involve intrinsic rewards, some extrinsic. Some are to do with outside pressures and accountability. Some relate to the satisfaction of writing and its value in aiding thinking. This chapter explores those reasons and the thinking behind them. It also discusses common reasons given for not publishing (or for not writing at all). The chapter ends by raising questions about the benefits and drawbacks of making one's writing public through traditional channels, questions that are revisited later in the book.

> I'm glad I did it, partly because it was worth doing, but mostly because I shall never have to do it again.
>
> (Mark Twain, circa 1900)

Motives for publishing: the whole gamut

Many people share Mark Twain's sentiments after they have finished the long, painful haul of writing and publishing a book or an article. But they still go on to do it again. Why?

In open discussion, people give a wide variety of reasons for wanting to publish. Over the last few years I have organized a number of seminars, often with students on our doctoral programmes, with the simple theme: why publish? The following reasons, in no particular order, have been put forward in these sessions:

- Career enhancement, improving the CV
- Getting promotion
- Sharing, communicating, disseminating, e.g. ideas, research findings, theory
- Filling a gap
- Joining the research community
- Vanity
- The Research Assessment Exercise for Universities (RAE)
- Responsibility, accountability

- Making an impact, making a difference – it may actually influence practitioners, policy makers/decision makers or just someone's thinking in an area
- Financial reward
- Publishing and dissemination being part of the ethics of responsible research
- Keeping issues alive, on the boil
- Setting up a dialogue
- Satisfaction
- Personal development
- Professional development
- Fun
- Raising awareness
- Earning respect or recognition, even fame and a 'reputation'
- Self-esteem and self-fulfilment
- Responding to someone
- Challenging a published viewpoint, belief, interpretation or orthodoxy
- Polemic
- Someone having told you that 'you've a good story to tell'
- Contributing to change and improvement
- Getting you to conferences in nice places.

These ideas form a good starting point for this chapter and for the book. Indeed, they cover most of the points in the literature. My own additional points, gleaned from the literature (such as Henson, 1999 or Thyer, 1994), are:

- To clarify your own thinking
- As part of the process of reflection
- As a way of interacting with others
- To earn respect or credibility
- To have the 'stamp of authority' or legitimation placed on your work
- To enhance your standing/position in your profession
- To give something back to your profession
- To increase your visibility
- To promote your department and enhance its profile.

These reasons could be classified, rather crudely, into *intrinsic* and *extrinsic* reasons; though, as we will see shortly, these two types of motivation are often hard to separate.

Why do people write? A range of voices

In writing this book, I interviewed twelve lecturers at different stages of their careers, with different types and quantities of publications in their track record, about their writing. Most of their comments are reported and discussed in

Chapter 3, on the writing process. Here I have included some of the lecturers' own thoughts on their motivation for writing. It seems that the desire to write is often intrinsically motivated whilst the motivation to publish is more extrinsically driven, but the two are often mixed. One expressed a belief that 'writing and researching can change things'. Another talked of 'prompts', from outside and inside:

> for example, 'I want to go to that conference – what could I do?' Or I may have a feeling that something has taken shape to the point where it can be presented in a fairly succinct form. Or the prompt may come from reading an article and thinking 'I could make a response to that', or the article helps to solidify some thoughts that were a bit vague before then.

> My professional writing stems from the responsibility I have to publish. I tend to see it as a staff-development activity as it refines my thinking and understanding, but it cannot be said that (a) writing comes easily, (b) I enjoy it or (c) I feel that I am particularly good at it. In terms of extrinsic motivation, it is true to say that you have more currency if you are writing and publishing in a particular area and that can be useful.

One intrinsic drive was that writing is

> a valuable process for marshalling ideas. I read a quote once about converting a 'puff of air' into something on a piece of paper, and writing does have that value of making you think through your ideas.

Similarly, one respondent told me:

> I write because writing gives a firmer shape to my ideas, clarifies thinking on new topics, synthesizes old patterns of work with the new data, theories or practices I am currently addressing. It pushes me to read more thoroughly and question what I read more critically. There is, for me, always a symbiotic relationship between reading and writing. They prompt and regulate one another. I usually write when I am invited to contribute after presenting a paper.

One interviewee broke his motivation down into areas:

- Because I'm teaching; I write both beforehand and after the teaching, about both the content and the process. Why? Because I want to keep developing the teaching and because I don't want to keep reinventing the wheel. Also, in good sessions new ideas emerge and I like to record them.
- Because I feel under some professional pressure to publish, though I don't feel this is particularly severe.

- Because I'm trying to construct a coherent story about learning and the nature of knowledge. I keep adding strands to my story by writing bits. None of this has been published, though I hope it will be one day.

One person, along with several others, called it 'a requirement of the job', a means of getting your name 'out there', a means to promotion, 'but within those constraints there is freedom to choose *what* I write – this freedom is reduced when it comes to targeting a journal'.

Most seem to be driven by a mixture of intrinsic and extrinsic motivation to write and publish:

> I know that writing is part of my job and so could say I do it because I HAVE to, but I was attracted to my university post because of the opportunities it offers for writing and discussing ideas for writing and research. I like to write because it stretches my mind; I enjoy playing with ideas and I never think as carefully about something as when I am writing. Because there is a need to carefully articulate and to structure, it forces me to think an idea through in greater detail. It also allows me to see and evaluate my ideas.

Similarly:

> In the case of book chapters, I write because I'm asked to. With regard to books and articles I will have an idea and feel the need to write about it. I'm not sure why! Just a desire to communicate, I suppose. Underlying everything are thoughts about the RAE and the need to produce. At ___ there was pressure to produce a minimum of three publications a year. These were reported in the University yearbook and fear of not having the requisite number of things to your name was compelling. It led to people writing for not very important publications – so didn't really achieve its goal! I still feel this imperative a bit.

> The answer at one level is quite simple. It's our job; it's the job of university academics to write. Writing is our work. But the question of why we write WHAT we write is a more complex one.

This respondent then went on to describe the field he writes in and the key debates in it, and said:

> We don't work as isolated individuals. I write with a sense of what the key issues are, what the unresolved problems and questions are, and try to make a contribution to the field, which will move the debate forward. So that's what makes me decide to write what I write about.

The same author spoke of the intrinsic motivation in writing:

> Through writing I develop more understanding – so it is a form of self-education, learning, development of understanding . . . that kind of thing. Besides, there is almost a Skinnerian re-inforcement to seeing your own work in print.

The responses show a range of motivations or prompts to write and publish. Some prompts might be called external: having a responsibility; the need for professional development; the desire for promotion; or simply being asked to write. Other prompts could be labelled 'internal': self-education, clarifying and refining one's thoughts, thinking through ideas, developing understanding and stretching the mind. It is clear from the quotations above that in considering motivation, we sometimes need to distinguish between writing and publishing. Many people suggest that the reason they write is to help them to think. Some of the really interesting authors on this area go further by saying that writing *is* thinking, or at least one form of thinking (Becker, 1986; Henson, 1999; Richardson, 1990). Wolcott (1990) puts it nicely by saying that 'writing is a way of gaining access to our own personal fund of information' (p. 22). It's as if by writing we dig up thoughts from somewhere in our minds that we didn't know were there. People in my interviews are saying the same thing – writing helps their thinking. They don't know what they really think until they start to (or try to) write. It relates to the old saying 'How do I know what I think until I see what I say?'

This kind of reason is given for writing per se. In Chapter 3 we look more fully at these themes by considering in more detail the writing process and how it relates to thinking and learning. But by its very nature, publishing (as opposed to writing for its own sake) is largely driven more by extrinsic factors and motives.

There are some interesting discussions in the literature of extrinsic motivation to publish. One very readable and pertinent discussion comes from Abby Day (Day, 1996). She gives eight good reasons for publishing that include some of those listed already: the desire for promotion, benefit to one's own institution, or to add to the body of knowledge in an area. She also talks of increasing one's own 'net worth' – to become a more 'sought-after person', someone more likely to be listened to. This is echoed in a point made by one of my own interviewees: 'You can't join in debates unless you write. And if you're not writing, your voice is not so important at a conference, because people don't know who you are.'

Day also points out that publishing allows us to revisit our own ideas and thoughts – once they are in print, we can look back on them (and perhaps have an inner chuckle or groan in some cases). Also, publishing allows us to get feedback on our thoughts and ideas from a much broader audience, e.g.

referees, eventual readers. This, of course, is at once the value of publishing and its potential to induce fear and apprehension.

Why not publish . . . or what puts people off?

I used another prompt in the seminars and discussions mentioned earlier by asking the converse: why not publish? As before, here is the list of points that came up, in no particular order:

- Lack of self-belief
- Lack of opportunities
- Embarrassment
- Not knowing what is expected of me, feeling that publishing is not appropriate for my role
- Fear of rejection
- Fear of being judged
- No track record
- Lack of know-how, time, motivation, energy
- Not knowing how to respond to criticism
- Knowing that you will have to wait for months for an answer
- Uncertainty
- Cost-benefit analysis coming out against submitting for publication
- Fear of exposure, vulnerability, putting one's head 'above the parapet'
- Fear of the work being superseded, becoming out-of-date
- Ethical reasons, e.g. fear of the work being misused or misapplied
- 'I'm not in the big boys' club'
- 'Am I good enough?'
- Will anyone ever read it? Will anyone be remotely interested?
- Editors' fashions, privileges, fads . . .
- Locating the right target.

Abby Day writes a valuable chapter (Day, 1996) on people's fears of publishing. She talks of the 'fear of being judged'; the thought that 'I'm a bad writer' or 'my work will be dismissed out of hand'. Other fears include: 'People will steal my ideas.' Apprehension about the process to which one is subjecting oneself by submitting a paper to a journal or any other refereeing process can be equally strong. Day talks of the feeling that 'It will be slated by referees' and the fear of the unknown, 'the black hole of refereeing and publishing' (p. 14). She suggests sitting down and recording exactly what your fears are and then considering each one in turn. In this book, I attempt to look at some of them, especially what she calls the 'black hole' that seems to swallow up our submissions, from which they emerge some weeks or even months later, with the addition of scathing comments or other forms of disparagement.

Another author (Dies, 1993) talks of the common obstacles or 'roadblocks' to publication. He starts by listing, rather dismissively, some of the 'groundless preoccupations' of potential authors such as 'doubts about their ability to write successfully, uncertainty about the worthiness of their ideas as judged by their professional colleagues and misunderstandings about the publication process'. My own view is that these are real rather than groundless. Ironically, Dies himself actually shows that they are genuine by reporting on his own empirical study (by questionnaire) of fifty experienced authors from different fields. His respondents listed a total of 118 perceived obstacles to publication, which he analysed by grouping them into four categories: personal apprehension, conceptual or organizational problems, difficulties relating to the submission of typescripts, and resource limitations.

Personal apprehension includes unsurprising feelings such as fear of rejection and self-doubt, with 'narcissism' and 'perfectionism' mentioned too. The latter category would include those who will not put pen to paper unless they can achieve a 'perfect outcome'. Dies uses the metaphor of 'stage-fright' to sum up this category. The second group involves more academic concerns. In my words: how does one develop a suitable and appropriate organizational framework for one's paper? Which topics should be included or excluded in order to keep a focus? Other worries are about keeping to the word limit and about writing style. The third area, 'submission problems', included three main sets of issues: finding the right journal, rewriting after referees' feedback and 'rebounding' after critical appraisal from reviewers. Dies' final category of perceived (and real) 'hurdles' involved resource limitations: lack of a mentor, lack of secretarial support and lack of time.

Factors that help people to publish

Dies' survey and discussion are actually helpful, and he goes on to offer useful practical advice to authors in preparing articles for submission and how to overcome commonly found problems in papers. My own view is that a concerted effort to remove some of the barriers listed above is the first stage in writing for publication. The main necessary (though not sufficient) condition for writing is to have, or be able to create, the time to do it. Given this necessary condition, other factors can be a major catalyst: the presence of encouraging, supportive colleagues; the assistance of a critical friend or friends; having one's confidence boosted; and finally, receiving concrete guidelines and advice on writing and publishing. The aim of later chapters in this book is to present and elaborate on these guidelines: to glean from various sources, and then to present evidence and advice on the presentation of material for publication with precisely the above fears and apprehensions in mind.

As an aside, my own personal apprehension, or more accurately a deterrent, to writing is quite simply that it's hard work – it requires effort, a struggle and some pain (see also Mullen, 2001). This is why I, and others, I'm sure, are so creative at inventing displacement activities.

The impostor syndrome

One of the reasons people give for not publishing, and I suffer from it myself, is what Brookfield (1995: 229) calls the 'impostor syndrome'. He discusses it in the context of teaching, but it is paralleled in writing. It is the feeling 'Am I teaching (writing) this under false pretences?' Do I really know what I'm talking about? The syndrome feeds on lack of confidence, fear of being 'found out' or of not being as competent as others might think we are, feelings of inadequacy, of not being worthy, fears of being revealed as a fraud, possession of an inferiority complex. Brookfield calls it one of the dangers of critically reflecting on our own practice.

For example, who am I to have the nerve to write this book? It is the first book I have written about writing. I don't have a degree in English literature (in fact, I barely scraped O-level English in 1966). I started my university education studying physics. And how many physicists can write? (Actually, a fair number, I suppose, if you consider Stephen Hawking, Fritzof Capra and Werner Heisenberg.) I've written quite a few books and articles, but maybe I've just been lucky? These are the kinds of thoughts that linger.

At its worst, the so-called syndrome can be inhibiting and create feelings of impotence and inferiority. This alone can be enough to stop people from exposing their writing. But, if brought into the open and shared, it can have a positive effect. It can lead to (or indeed is a feature of) a sense of humility, of recognizing one's own limitations. One concrete outcome for me is that I always try to read as much as is available on a subject before attempting to do my own writing (the problem with this, however, is knowing when to stop reading and start writing). Not only that, think of the opposite to the impostor syndrome: conceit, a superiority complex, super-confident assertion, lack of reflection, incaution, the kind of brash over-confidence that some people in academic and political life seem to have been imbued with, i.e. the ability to speak confidently and sound knowledgeable on any subject, even if they know nothing about it.

Outside pressures: has the RAE (Research Assessment Exercise) had an impact?

Many people feel that the RAE has had a large impact on the way people publish, the 'targets' they aim for and the quantity of publications coming into the world. Yet there is not a huge amount of empirical evidence to support intuition, anecdote and common-room discussion. One study in 2000 (Talib, 2000) did cover an impressive sample of 130 editors from a range of disciplines, asking for their views on the impact of the RAE. The data from the 72 responses

(55 per cent of the total) were hardly conclusive. Of the editors responding, about 43 per cent thought that the RAE had increased the volume of sub-missions prior to the deadline, 22 per cent thought not, and 35 per cent were not sure.

From the more general findings, some salient points were: the RAE had not resulted in more co-authorship, in the views of the editors; there seemed to be an increase in the number of Ph.D. students submitting papers before their degree had been examined; and many editors felt that 'academics do try to milk as many papers as possible from the same project', perhaps as a result of the RAE. Some editors felt that 'pressure to publish' has increased the number of journals now in circulation – it may also have increased turn-around time. The general view was that the RAE has *not improved quality*.

Elton (2000) makes similar points about the RAE, though more from personal experience than from an empirical base such as Talib's. Elton argues that the first exercise (in 1992) resulted in 'a proliferation of new journals' and also the publication of 'essentially the same work' in different guises in different outlets. (His son Ben, incidentally, might well have described these ploys more comically and satirically.) Similarly, it led to the 'splitting up of research papers into several smaller ones' (p. 276). Elton's view was that the 1992 exercise, by exerting pressure to get published in the short term, 'dis-advantaged long term research'. Some of these 'bad practices' were, Elton argues, corrected by changes in the conduct of the 1996 RAE.

But one of the lasting effects seems to be a greater pressure and bias towards publication in academic, refereed journals rather than 'professional and more popular journals' (incidentally, many professional journals are refereed, which Elton does not point out). His conclusion, which I would agree with, is that the RAEs have reinforced 'academic traditionalism', encouraged short-termism, and stifled new developments.

Finally, one amusing comment made by a journal editor I interviewed was that, as a Research Assessment Exercise becomes imminent, some academics actually phone the editor asking if their contribution could be brought forward in the queue. We look again at this idea of queue jumping in Chapter 4 on the editorial process.

Past complaints about academic publications

It is worth devoting a short section at this early stage in the book to some of the complaints which have been published about publications. The examples here are drawn from the field of education. There seemed to be a short, sharp phase at the end of the 1990s (mainly 1996–1999) when it became fashionable to criticize educational research and the publications stemming from it. In par-ticular, Hargreaves (1996) and Tooley and Darby (1998) were the main snipers, with ammunition or at least encouragement from parts of the media and the now legendary former chief of Ofsted, Chris Woodhead (see Woodhead, 1997).

Their publications, and a rather more measured report by Hillage *et al.* (1998), presented a number of criticisms of educational publishing, largely in the so-called academic journals. Taken collectively, the accusations were that much of the output of research in education is: irrelevant to practitioners and policy makers; non-cumulative, i.e. not building upon existing literature or knowledge; inaccessible and exclusive; unreadable and poorly written, or impenetrable; biased and partisan (see Wellington, 2000: 166–173 for a full discussion).

Many of these criticisms came from Tooley and Darby (1998), who examined (in a very partisan, biased way, as is the tendency with human beings) forty-one articles from four different journals. Their report provoked a strong reaction at the time and is still worth reading in full. Its main tenets were as follows: only a small minority of the articles took a detached, 'non-partisan approach'; many had methodological flaws, e.g. lack of triangulation, bias in sampling; presentation was poor and many did not include important factual details such as sample size and sampling criteria; many articles were only tenuously con-nected with policy and practice; 'a picture emerged' of researchers doing their work largely 'in a vacuum, unheeded and un-noticed by anyone else' (p. 6).

One of their specific criticisms, which I have some sympathy with, was that certain authors in education journals have a tendency to include names of the great and the good from fields such as post-modernism for no other reason than to bolster their paper or to give it an air of intellectualism. Names such as Bourdieu, Lyotard, Derrida and Foucault tend to appear at the drop of a hat (or, in the case of Schrödinger, the drop of a cat). Similarly, certain types of theory sometimes seem to be thrown in as a ploy to reinforce the research and give it legitimacy.

We will look at some of their complaints later in the book in considering the role of and rationale for peer review, and also the criteria by which journal editors and their referees allegedly judge submitted papers. Since all the papers judged by Tooley and Darby had been peer reviewed, what does this tell us about the process?

So – why publish?

The main answer I would give to university lecturers, though it might sound elitist, hard-nosed and pompous, is that 'it's part of the job'. One of my brothers is a carpenter. During his apprenticeship he learnt to do various things such as fitting windows, laying wooden floors and hanging doors. He would get short shrift on a building site if he told the employer 'I'm a carpenter, but by the way I don't hang doors.' Lecturers sometimes say 'Well, I'd love to publish, but I don't have time because of too much teaching and admin.' My answer is that this is equivalent to carpenters saying that they don't hang doors. Publish-ing comes with the job – it is not some sort of hobby or sideline that some people somehow find time for. If one does 'not have the time', then (as the union leaders used to say) a 'full and frank exchange' with the head of department is needed to create it. Time needs to be given to people to write, assuming that it is part of the job. Time is a necessary (though often not a sufficient) condition for writing and publishing to take place. Time for writing has to be 'managed', by both managers and individuals.

This applies to university lecturers. However, the reasons and motives for others to publish are many and varied, as we have seen in this chapter. Students, teachers, and freelance or professional researchers will have some or all of the motives presented above.

And finally – what did publishers ever do for us (authors)?

Some researchers and writers might well be tempted to go it alone in seeking to make their work public and disseminate their hard-worked-for piece of writing. This is increasingly possible given the World Wide Web and the Internet as a platform for expressing and spreading ideas and findings. Indeed, some editorial boards have actually divorced themselves from commercial publishers who may be overcharging for subscriptions or simply getting in the way, and set up their own, autonomous e-journals. Prior to the advent of e-publishing the opportunities for authors to go their own way were limited to self-publishing or kitchen-table publishing – or, in some cases, vanity publishing, in which a publisher is paid to take on work, produce it and disseminate it.

So, it is worth stopping to consider what contribution publishers of books or journals make to the overall furtherance of education and scholarship. Firstly, they can offer improved presentation of one's work – in terms of what is still called 'typesetting', attractive jackets and binding and generally improved appearance and layout. Secondly, journals in particular offer *archiving to your writing*: if your article appears in a journal it becomes part of an archive, perhaps stretching back a long way. You become part of a series, with a track record and a history. For example, I recently wrote an article for a professional journal for its 300th edition, and this gave me more satisfaction than writing a book. Thirdly, the traditional publication process (book or journal) offers improved content and enhanced quality. A journal effectively gives you free feedback (even if it is painful) on your writing. It also provides editing, copy-editing and proofreading. Fourthly, the process offers improved publicity and marketing: publishers have links and networks with the academic community, librarians, library suppliers, bookshops and booksellers. How many kitchen-table authors could claim the same links? Publishers' links, of course, provide far better distribution and therefore dissemination of your work. Next, traditional publishing offers enhanced status to the author, which vanity or kitchen-table publishing could not (and this may be true of electronic publishing, as we discuss in the final chapter). The fact that your work has been through an editorial and review process gives it some mark of quality and authority. Finally, commercial publishers offer some degree of protection of an author's material from potential offenders. For example, the publisher will observe and enforce copyright law and is usually able to take legal action if work is pirated or plagiarized (Hills, 1987: 38).

In summary, publishers can provide improved presentation, content, dissemination and marketing, and publishing can enhance kudos, and will protect and archive your material. For all these reasons, the traditional channels of publication, i.e. of making one's work public, bestow huge advantages. They also carry a cost, in terms of energy and time and being subjected to a review process that may be lengthy, painful and in some cases allegedly less than fair – these are issues we look at in later chapters.

Chapter 2

What might you publish about?

People's writing is published in all kinds of forms and media, in various shapes and sizes, ranging from newspaper letters to extensive journal articles through to major books. This chapter explores the subject matter that has formed the basis for academic publications. The chapter also discusses the different 'levels' at which people may write, often based on the same area of thought or research.

The whole gamut of possibilities . . .

As an advance organizer, this chapter starts with a list of many of the possibilities for the subject matter of a proposed publication:

- A research study (content)
  Interim results
  'Flagging it up' (seeking suggestions or collaborators)
  Final results
  Ideas for further research
  Seeking feedback on any of the above
- A research study (process)
  Innovative methods
  New methodology or approach
  Practical issues in carrying out the research
- A (new) teaching approach
- A curriculum development (preferably with evaluation of the above two – action research?)
- A response, rejoinder or critique of already published work
- A non-empirical survey/analysis of a field of research or debate
  A literature review
  A meta-analysis
- A philosophical discussion or critique; a conceptual analysis (cf. John Locke's notion of the labourer clearing away some of the undergrowth)
- An opinion piece or a comment, e.g. for *TES* or *THES*
- A book review.

What to publish about and when?

The list above shows that a wide range of possibilities of 'what to write about' is available. One of the key questions for new writers is: how do I make a start? Where should I aim in getting a foot on the ladder? Many people start with a book review, an opinion piece, or a similar special section in a journal that may not be as heavily refereed as (say) a full-blown journal article. As we see in a later chapter, some journals have designated sections for newer writers or in some cases students – these may be called 'Current issues', 'Signposts' or 'Viewpoints', for example. Journals may also encourage people to publish at different stages of a research project or study. Simply 'flagging up' interest in an area and attempting to delineate the key area for research, the burning questions or the possible research methodology or even methods may form the theme of an article. Interim results or even the outcome of a pilot study may form good subject matter. By publishing at these early stages, authors can indicate their interest and, it is hoped, link with or engage with others in that field. Effectively, writers are saying 'Here I am: this is what I am doing and planning to do; can you help or can I join the community?' To achieve this respectably (and be 'cumulative') an author would have to recognize previous work in the area and point to new directions, new theoretical perspectives, questions, methods/approaches, or lines of research. More conventionally, many people wait until the end of a research project or study and then present their findings. My argument here is that it may not always be necessary to wait until this phase. Research students would be well advised to discuss their exact strategy for getting started in publishing with their supervisor.

In deciding what to publish about, a key point to note is that many studies have both a findings or content element that is worth publishing for its importance or impact *and* a methodological component. It may well be that a research study merits the publication of two types of paper or book chapter: one on the results and their implications, the other on the methodology or even the actual methods employed and their advantages and drawbacks.

One important type of article is the reply, response, rejoinder or critique of an existing article (some in this category, incidentally, are written by a chosen author, invited by the editor, but this need not deter unsolicited submissions). I have deliberately avoided including the old word 'polemic' here (according to the *OED*, it derives from the Greek word for 'war', *polemos*). The word's meaning varies according to its users, but generally means 'aggressive controversy' as a noun and 'disputatious' or 'warlike' as an adjective; it can mean a 'controversialist' in describing a person (originally a theologian, circa 1680, according to the *OED*). My view is that polemic, in its traditional sense, is best avoided. One of the motives for publishing for many writers is the desire to engage in public debate and discussion, and to further a field by so doing. However, this is not the same thing as engaging in polemics. The latter is likely to create enemies rather than critical friends and create heat rather than light – something that most people new to publishing could do without. Anyway, who wants to be known as a 'polemicist'?

As mentioned in Chapter 1, past criticisms of educational research have included (Hargreaves, 1996; Tooley and Darby, 1998) the accusation that it is not cumulative, i.e. it does not build upon and respond to earlier work. However, this does not necessitate that it should be polemic by nature.

Stories or narrative-style articles may well be welcomed by some book publishers or journal editors. Such articles may take a case-study approach, e.g. an account of the creation of a new course or the closure of a department or a school, the 'story' of an Ofsted inspection, or a narrative of how a central policy was put into practice and taken over (the term 'hi-jacked' has been used here) by practitioners. All of these narratives can be of wide interest to both practitioners and researchers.

Many new authors first get into print as a result of doing their thesis, for a Master's degree, a diploma or a doctorate (Ed.D. or Ph.D.). Some theses will form the basis of an article or perhaps two or more, e.g. one on the findings and how they were arrived at, another on the methodological approach if it is novel or original. One of the dilemmas that students face is whether to publish any of their work *before* the Master's or doctoral thesis has been submitted. There are no hard and fast rules on this. As a supervisor and an internal and external examiner I have seen many Ph.D. students publish aspects of their work (occasionally co-authored with their supervisor, which raises other issues) before the thesis has been examined. My own personal experience is that this has not presented a problem for examiners, but I would suggest to students that they discuss this carefully with their supervisor before going ahead.

Some theses have formed the ideal basis for a book. One author I particularly admire in achieving this is Janice Edwards (1994). She succeeded in turning her M.Ed. thesis, based on detailed case studies of eight dyslexic students, into an interesting and well-written book for Cassell (now Continuum). This is no mean task. The author is writing for a different audience (the book market, as opposed to examiners), and difficult decisions have to be made about what to omit from a thesis (especially a large Ph.D.). For example, large sections of the literature review and the methodology discussion, both essential in writing a thesis that has to be defended, will need to be shaved down. And not least, the title may need changing, partly to appeal to the book's potential market (in Edwards' case, to *The Scars of Dyslexia*).

Those with a heavy involvement in and commitment to teaching need not run short of potential areas worth writing and publishing (and researching) about. New forms and media for learning, for example, are widely reported and the reports widely read. Developments in electronically based learning and teaching (e-learning) are currently one focus of attention. In the past, descriptions of new teaching methods, new curricula or new models of learning have quite rightly been widely published. Some of this has come under the banner of 'Action Research' (see Wellington, 2000 for some discussion), but this need not be the only forum for presenting and discussing learning and teaching approaches in print. The correct outlet or target for such writing may be a 'professional journal' rather than an academic one, but this boundary is blurring (see later chapters on targeting writing).

As Eggleston and Klein (1997: 2) point out, the organization, management and administration of teaching can also be an area that *deserves* to be written about and published. New features of initial teacher education such as mentoring in schools provide fertile areas for discussion, empirical research and critique. Any writing for publication, whatever the area, should in some sense be 'newsworthy' and original, i.e. worth making public. Many people in education have something worth writing about and making public.

Finally, it is comforting to consider that there are numerous ways to be original. Phillips and Pugh (1994) give an encouraging list of fifteen different possibilities – this is a reassuring check-list to consult, for writers at any level (see Box 2.1).

Box 2.1 Fifteen ways of being original

- Setting down a major piece of new information in writing for the first time
- Continuing a previously original piece of work
- Carrying out original work designed by a senior colleague
- Providing a single original technique, observation or result in an otherwise unoriginal but competent piece of research
- Having many original ideas, methods and interpretations all performed by others under the direction of the writer
- Showing originality in testing somebody else's idea
- Carrying out empirical work that hasn't been done before
- Making a synthesis that hasn't been made before
- Using already known material but with a new interpretation
- Trying out something in this country that has previously only been done in other countries
- Taking a particular known technique and applying it in a new area
- Bringing new evidence to bear on an old issue
- Being cross-disciplinary and using different methodologies
- Looking at areas that people in the discipline haven't looked at before
- Adding to knowledge in a way that hasn't previously been done before

---

Source: Phillips and Pugh (1994)

An analysis of journal content: categories of writing for journals

In considering what one might write about, another angle is to examine a range of journals in order to see the types of article or other piece that they publish.

The ESRC study by Packwood *et al.* (1997) closely examined three journals at that time: the *British Educational Research Journal (BERJ)*, the *British Journal of Psychology (BJP)* and *Sociology*. Only the first could be considered a mainstream education journal, although the latter two may be read, and written for, by people in the education field. Given the stated aims of each journal it is not surprising that each had a slightly different focus. However, they also had several common features in their contents. All three contained critiques of research and of theory, all contained 'discursive' articles, all contained responses to critiques and all contained articles on theoretical and philosophical perspectives (most commonly in *Sociology*). All the journals contained reports of empirical work based on primary sources, with the *BJP* having the highest percentage of this genre (78 per cent) and *BERJ* the second highest (53 per cent of all its papers). Notably, reports on 'action research' were only present in *BERJ*. The authors concluded that the *BERJ* articles reflect its 'eclectic, multi-disciplinary approach'. The ESRC study went on to analyse (again quantitatively) the methodological approach and actual methods used in each of the three selected journals. Case-study methodology was far more prevalent in *BERJ*, while the quantitative/experimental approach was, unsurprisingly, very common in *BJP*, with over half of its articles in this paradigm (only 4 per cent in *BERJ*). As for actual methods, all three journals published articles with so-called 'mixed methods', but this mode of data collection was most common in *BERJ*. The use of tests to collect data was, predictably, far more prevalent in *BJP* than in the other two. The use of longitudinal studies was far more common in *BERJ* (30 per cent as opposed to *BJP*'s 8 per cent). The focus of attention or population for research in each journal varied, with schoolchildren and school staff making up over half of *BERJ*'s focus, whilst *BJP* articles seemed to concentrate on undergraduates and 'patients' – a clear case, perhaps, of access being the all-important factor in empirical research? The bias in *Sociology* was clearly towards research involving adults. Finally, methods of data analysis vary widely. *BERJ* articles included mostly qualitative analysis and 'mixed methods', although as the ESRC report authors point out, there is no single dominant model since statistical analysis was also well used. Not surprisingly, *BJP* involved largely statistical analysis (in 87 per cent of all its articles), with *Sociology* having a much more eclectic approach.

These data are interesting although they focus only on three journals, and the emphases may have changed since 1997, along with the journals. The general point to be made from all this is that it is well worth the author's while to study the track record or past contents of a journal for its bias in terms of its content, its methodological bias and the actual methods used in data collection and analysis.

My own, very recent, interviews with editors of journals show that a wide range of categories of writing can be submitted to them, much wider than the traditional view of the 'refereed journal article'. For example, journals may include letters, book reviews and review essays, 'Viewpoints' (short statements of opinion, argument or counter-argument), Colloquia (sections of 400–900 words reporting, perhaps, work in progress, brief stories of a project or a reaction to a previous contribution), editorials, and other categories. It is well worth looking at some of the websites of the major journals to remind ourselves that submissions need not be confined to the traditional 4,000–6,000-word article. Many of the writers I have interviewed 'got started' or 'put their feet on the first rung of the ladder' by writing a review, a short essay or a viewpoint. However, the way they may be viewed in an assessment exercise also needs to be remembered, as we discuss shortly.

Hierarchies and levels: writing for different audiences

The main purpose of writing and publishing research is to communicate with other people. It is hardly worth doing research if it is not disseminated. Communication can, and should, take place with a number of different audiences in mind: one's peers and fellow-researchers, practitioners, policy makers, curriculum planners and developers, teachers or lecturers, parents or the general public. The ground rule here is surely horses for courses: 'Different purposes and different audiences require different styles of writing' (Woods, 1999: 48). In addition, different aims and audiences require different *lengths* of writing. Figure 2.1 shows possible examples of different 'platforms' for writing, of different lengths for different audiences.

An interesting author on 'writing for diverse audiences' is Richardson (1985, 1987 and 1990). From a piece of research on single women in relationships with married men, she published both academic journal articles and a popular book (*The New Other Woman*). Peter Woods (1999: 48–50) discusses the way she varied her language, her style, her tone and the structure of her writing for different audiences. Woods himself gives an example of writing for different audiences from his own research into 'critical events' in schools. This was disseminated via an academic journal article focusing on the theory emerging from the research; another journal article concentrating on the pupils' perspectives, including case-study material; and a reader for students training to be primary teachers with a catchy title including the term 'exceptional educational events'. The student reader included only eight references; the academic article contained over one hundred.

One of my own experiences relating to Figure 2.1 has been to convert my own Ph.D. thesis into a book (Wellington, 1989, on the links between education

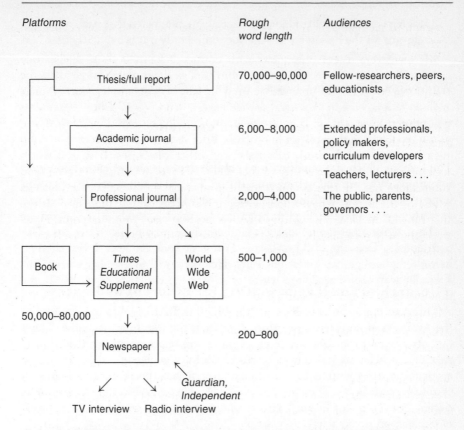

Figure 2.1 Publishing for different audiences (adapted from Wellington, 2000)

and employment). The book (about 60,000 words long) was considerably shorter than the thesis (about 100,000 words including all the appendices). The book omitted large chunks of qualitative data and most of the discussion on methodology which appeared in the thesis.

Book proposals require considerable thought partly because, unlike theses, books have to be sold, which means that somebody must want to buy them (see Chapter 5). My experience with publishers and their commissioning editors is that they are extremely helpful and will support a good idea even if it will not result in tens of thousands of copies being sold.

However, all the while authors subject to assessment exercises need to be conscious of steering the right course between audience appeal and scholarly substance. The RAE overview panel for the 2001 exercise commented:

> While it is accepted that those working in the area of education have pressure on them to write books and articles in the form of guidance for

teachers or other practitioners, it has to be remembered that such writing is relevant for the research assessment exercise only if it is explicitly based on research.

We return to this issue in Chapter 5 on book publishing.

The RAE and what counts as an 'eminent, academic' publication?

The level at which you might wish to publish depends almost entirely on your intentions. Why are you writing something? Who is it aimed at? What do you hope to achieve by publishing it? In David Lodge's novel *Nice Work*, the heroine (a fairly new and prolific English literature lecturer) is watched by her partner as she is writing her latest book on eighteenth-century female novelists. The partner asks, 'Does the world really need another book on dead novelists?' The heroine replies: 'probably not, but I do'. Her book will further her career – in a similar way, many academics write to satisfy the demands of the RAE, for themselves and for their departments.

This does not mean that every article which is 'RAE-able' (a term coined in the 1990s) is of no interest or value other than the assessment exercise. Many outputs cited for the RAE are of great value and importance. But the point is that such articles are unlikely to be read by a huge audience – they tend to be academic articles written for an academic audience (peers, other researchers or research students). They are probably not targeted, quite rightly, at practitioners or even policy makers. This is why an awareness of the different levels of publication is valuable.

The act of writing for an 'eminent academic journal' does not prevent the same author from publishing work at other levels and communicating with user groups: RAE writing and user-group writing are not mutually exclusive. Writers can deliberately aim their writing at different levels of publication (see Figure 2.1). The overview report of the 2002 RAE stated that people from higher-scoring departments 'typically published in eminent academic journals, book chapters *and* outlets providing significant interaction with the education community more generally'.

This statement of course raises the question What is an eminent academic journal? Is there a hierarchy? On what is it based? Are there any explicit, agreed criteria for 'eminence', or do they all lie in the eye of the beholder? These questions are considered in Chapter 4, which examines the business of writing, editing and refereeing for journals.

Chapter 3

Writing and the writing process

Writing is one of those experiences, painful for many, which people don't often talk about. The writing process is commonly regarded as something that adults go away and do in private (only school pupils seem to have to do it publicly). However, a lot of useful material has been written about writing. This chapter looks at writing and the writing process, drawing primarily on my own interviews with a range of people who have published, still do, and can reflect back on it, sometimes with humour.

The process of writing a research paper

My own trawl of the literature has revealed few detailed and helpful reflections on the writing process when publication is the goal. One excellent exception was written by David Bridges (Bridges, 1999), who chronicled his own experiences of writing a research paper over a nine-month period. Bridges comes up with some useful hints and suggestions: openly seek advice and sources of references from colleagues (by e-mail and face to face); timetable spaces for intensive bursts of active writing; in between these, keep a file, box or notebook for occasional ideas, thoughts or notes that occur during 'low-activity' periods. He talks of three levels of activity: high, low and inactivity. He suggests that during periods of low or inactivity the writer should use the file or notebook to record thoughts that occur while walking the dog (if you don't have one, lying in the bath will do). Bridges also talks, as have many other authors and interviewees in my study, of the need for a kind of gestation period when you leave the writing alone, coming back to it with a fresh approach. This is rather like Day's idea (Day, 1996) of allowing the right-hand side of the brain (the intuitive side as opposed to analytical) to take over for a while (see also Dorothea Brande, 1983).

Reflections on the writing process

Bridges' introspections and his willingness to publish them are interesting and valuable. My own, less brave approach has been to interview twelve (six male, six female) of my colleagues, all of whom write and publish as part of their job

and many of whom seem to gain intrinsic rewards from writing. Some colleagues are highly experienced and have written books and articles that are known (and have been translated) worldwide. Others are no less able but are less experienced and have fewer publications to their name. Most interviews were conducted face to face, although some were sent and received by e-mail. The interview schedule is shown in Appendix 1. Here I report some of their responses under the headings used as a rough structure for the interviews.

Planning, thinking and writing

Different people adopt different approaches to planning, and sometimes different approaches are used by the same writers. The way we plan, structure and organize our writing will clearly depend on its purpose and its intended audience. Below I give my own selection, with little comment, from some of the data:

> I like to write to a plan. I produce section headings and fairly detailed jottings about what these will contain and then follow them through. These I write in red pen (a very particular type of pen – Staedler stick – from a supply that I amassed when I worked for ___ – it's possible that when I run out I'll never write anything again) – on scrap paper. Sometimes I find that the plan isn't working so I revise it – I never write without an outline to my side, though.
>
> (female)

> I do plan my writing, but I usually find that in the process of writing the plan might take a new direction. I will then 'go with the flow'. My plan is something I produce after I have hand written lots of ideas and questions in a very shorthand way. Sometimes I have structured the writing of an article around overheads that I produced for a presentation – either for teaching students or for my peers. I realized that OHTs [overhead transparencies] are a bit like a plan only more detailed because they include quotations and the most important findings from data.
>
> (female)

> I have ideas in the back of my mind, but I only really know what I want to say as I begin to write things down. That drives me into more reading and re-reading of my own texts. Sometimes in the middle of writing one section I get an idea for another part which I don't want to lose so I jot down a heading – perhaps a couple of key words – perhaps it's a quote from a book I am reading. I can sometimes switch between sections in this way letting one section be while ideas form round another point. I rarely write the proper introduction until I have finished. My writing

process is messy and non-linear but excites me. I perhaps can fall into over implicit connections. I disobey all those instructions we give students about signposting intentions.

(female)

I usually pre-plan it, though on the occasions when I've just let it 'flow' it seems to have worked quite well. The more sure I am of the theme the more natural it would be to let it flow, at least on first draft. I think I do a lot of thinking beforehand, but invariably the act of writing is creative for me – some new links and strands pop up. I think I do structure my writing, though the structure often gets revised.

(male)

One respondent talked of her thinking reaching a certain level and then 'the iceberg breaks out into open water'. She continued: 'I'm awful at planning . . . it's more about starting to write and seeing where it leads me.' Her view was that she has problems with 'linearity'. 'Writing feels a bit like "plaiting" together ideas. It's not necessarily one idea done, then onto the next idea. They might run through in separate streams, then every so often they get caught together and plaited.'

Another (female) author told me: 'I haven't yet found the template for perfect writing. The secret algorithm hasn't arrived yet.' She talked of using reading to help create or suggest headings and sub-headings that could then act as hooks. Reading 'gives you a feel for what the "hooks" are, and at least gives you some key headings for what you're writing. Sometimes I read until I find the hook really. Then I do try to make a structure, which I'm hopeless at. It becomes a bit of a magical mystery tour.'

Two male authors are self-confessed pre-planners:

I always plan before I start to write. I've developed fairly fixed ideas about the way I structure my writing. I can apply this structure to different kinds of writing (a sort of generalizable structure).

I'm very much at one end of the scale here. I spend a lot of time on planning and structuring before I start. I have a very strong structure which arises just from thinking and reading. Of course, as I start writing, that structure will change. But basically I put a lot of emphasis on pre-planning and particularly on structure, because the nature of what I write is argumentative. So I need the structure of the argument mapped out – and I work to this map. But quite often I don't actually, myself, understand fully what the argument is until I've done the first draft. So the first draft is often a learning curve. [The interview revealed that he also asks students whom he supervises to work the same way.]

And finally, from a female writer:

> I plan things visually, with a spidergram. I brainstorm ideas, then try to connect them with a spidergram or a mind map. The only danger with that is that I try to throw everything in. I do lots of drafts of these and throw plenty of them in the bin. I find that as I'm writing the plan changes. If I write under sub-headings it's easier to move things. I can cut and paste, or move things to the bottom of the page if I don't know where to put them.

The actual writing process

People seem to vary widely in how they actually write, what they write with and how they put their writing together: 'I write in chunks and then lash them together. I produce several drafts all word-processed' (male).

> I usually write using pen and paper. I may not write from 'beginning to end'; the structure helps here – if I have a map of the 'landscape' of the topic I feel OK about wandering about in one part of the map and then starting a new journey in another part.
>
> (male)

> I adore my word processor. I love the possibility of completing fragments and introducing new ideas from other pieces of writing I am engaged in. My work is like patch work or quilting rather than weaving. I am constantly bringing disparate ideas into conjunction with one another. I love to be able to write at speed and correct, amend and refine at leisure.
>
> (female)

> When I've started writing something I do have to run through it from the beginning to get to where I was, which is why the first parts of everything I write are so much better than the endings. I do it all (composing) at the keyboard now – I never thought I would because I used to like my paper – but there are points when I actually have to print it and spread the pages out so that I can sort of see the shape of it. I do sometimes think: 'oh, that's a really nice paragraph but it doesn't fit'. But it's too nice to lose, so I just stick it at the bottom of the document and may retrieve it at a later stage.
>
> (female)

> Cut and paste was invented for me. I start off with headings, or bits, or sections (whatever they're called) . . . and I share things under all those different headings and bits. I then start shifting things around. Half of my

writing time is spent cutting and pasting. I'm always printing things out and putting arrows and hand-written stuff on it.

(female)

I write very much in sections at a time, from beginning to end. I find that using pen on paper is much more 'organic' in terms of the relationship between thinking and writing. It's almost going down your arm, from your head, and onto the paper. [He writes on wide-lined paper, every second line, writes 500–600 words, then goes through it and scribbles in the spaces, changing, adding and pruning.] What you end up with looks terrible – but you know it's a first draft. But if you do that on a computer it comes out looking great – but it's still a first draft. It looks better than it is. But with hand-written stuff, it actually is better than it looks. I always produce many drafts – I don't think I've ever published anything which hasn't gone through a minimum of about seven drafts, and sometimes as many as fifteen. Gradually, the changes get less and less. I never write at work.

(male)

Writing with a word processor has given me more confidence and flexibility. I'm not afraid to delete things I've written and start again.

(female)

I write from beginning to end. I have tried, when things aren't going well, to do out-of-sequence bits first, but I feel uncomfortable and it doesn't work for me. I produce loads of drafts and have to read through everything I've written every time I sit down and start again. This means that some days I don't produce anything new – I revise what I already had. I think I am painfully slow. I agonize over every word and phrase. Many is the day when I have worked for ten hours and only produced a paragraph that I'm satisfied with. I write straight on to the word processor – although – as I've said – I produce a red-pen plan.

(female)

Getting feedback

Most interviewees (along with Bridges, 1999, cited above) feel that feedback, time for reflection and redrafting are vitally important in the writing process. Some people like to try things out with students, or at a seminar or at a conference. Many seek a critical friend or colleague to give feedback:

I choose people who I know will understand the sort of work I'm into, will be critical, but will be constructive and positive too.

(male)

In collaborative work it's an ongoing thing. But when I'm writing alone I do ask someone who is familiar with the area to cast an eye. I also ask a friend who is not an academic to do a bullshit check. He will point out convoluted and jargon and 'academic' language (which I try very hard not to use anyway, but the odd bit slips through sometimes). I'm usually defensive at first about comments – but then come back to them and see that the writer probably had a point!

(female)

I like sometimes to keep my work to myself, especially if I fear the criticism of someone who might exert an authority over my text. In collaboration with a partner I love the exchange of ideas, the struggle for joint meaning, etc. I do like sharing with a careful reader who spots gaps in my text's argument.

(female)

I always ask for feedback and I always react positively. I think it is foolish to release our writing on the academic readership without first putting it past some critical friends. I would choose a sympathetic reader who had knowledge in the field or, in the case of something destined for a practitioner clientele, I might ask a typical 'consumer'.

(male)

Feedback is essential for me, even if I don't always take on what is fed back! What I look for is someone who I think can engage with the topic and can judge it from the point of view of possible audiences.

(male)

Occasionally, I would go to somebody who *didn't* think in the same way as I did, just to get a completely different perspective.

(female)

I like to share my writing with people. I like to share my writing with colleagues that I can trust. I want usable feedback, not people who are going to be horrible to me. I often require different feedback from different colleagues.

(female)

One person explained that she is keen to get feedback from a colleague with a totally different approach to research methodology, e.g. quantitative. This raised questions and posed challenges:

> I'm not precious about my writing, but on the other hand you can feel vulnerable when you go public, so I'm slightly wary. But I like people who are honest; I don't want flattery.
>
> (female)

Feedback from external sources, such as referees, is seen as more of a problem:

> As far as referees' comments are concerned, I get very disappointed. I have put in the bin many responses and not returned to the article again! But when I confessed this to a colleague she explained that in fact the articles I had binned would probably have been published if I had attended to the suggestions given. I honestly had no idea of this at the time.
>
> (female)

> Referees' comments are a pain when they appear to reflect a strong bias in a referee's 'take' on the topic: e.g. I recall submitting a paper to a journal and getting feedback from a self-declared committed positivist about an article that was arguing that other ways of looking at 'evidence' and argument were appropriate. Frustrating! It would have been better to have had a different referee – probably I should have submitted to a different journal, I guess.
>
> (female)

> I hate it [feedback], unless it's glowing, of course. I get really angry when you write something for a journal and you get something back which almost takes it to task for *not* doing something which you *didn't* set out to do in the first place. One referee accused me of being a *gadfly* because I'd actually gone across several different topics . . . and I took exception to that. So I looked up the provenance of the term 'gadfly' and it actually fitted in with some of the imagery I was trying to use in the paper. So I incorporated the referee's comments into the paper and made it a kind of 'peg' for the paper . . . and I felt that I got my own back as well!
>
> (female)

On negative feedback:

> It does knock your confidence and I don't know if there's a gender thing around that. But immediately I get negative feedback my first thought is: 'Oh God, I'm not good enough.' The shock bit and feeling of inadequacy

is the first thing – then I have to try and put that to one side so that I can work with it.

(female)

I've always found comments from referees very useful, but very often uncomfortable. Referees seem to have very different views on whether their comments are summative or formative. The least satisfactory are comments rejecting an article but not giving detailed feedback on *why*.

(male)

One interviewee chooses journals very carefully to minimize her chances of negative feedback:

It's important for me if referees have picked up the weaknesses that I can see and I can agree with. If they'd picked on things that I cherish dearly then I probably would be very upset.

Another (female) writer found it very 'comforting' to go on a course run by an eminent author who showed people a paper of hers that had been rejected, and the referees' comments on it. She told her own story of receiving two very different responses from two referees on one of her articles: one very supportive, one very critical (she suspected that one was from a male, the other a female). She did not re-do the article, partly because 'I was moving on very quickly at that point as well.'

The collaborative writing process

Many people write collaboratively, and this can be an interesting process. My interviewees made several pertinent comments on it. It can pose problems if authors have totally different writing styles or don't work in similar ways. On the other hand, it can be exciting. The general mode of working seems to be that co-authors write separate sections or chapters on their own, then read each other's work and piece it together. Several seem to find collaboration enjoyable and to add value ('two minds are better than one'). However, I did not find any writers who actually write together either with pen and paper or, like two pianists, at the same keyboard looking at the same computer screen.

Collaborative writing? I enjoy this. I don't think I'm especially detached from my writing . . . and so someone else's take on the ideas is reassuring and makes me feel that the writing is less likely to be idiosyncratic.

(male)

I find writing a lonely business and prefer to collaborate. I prefer to brainstorm and then go off and write my part, as time spent formulating can be time wasted.

(male)

Usually when writing with a partner we agree a general framework but designate separate responsibilities for chapters. We write in step with each other, swapping texts for comments, leaving gaps where we think the other might contribute something more. Finally we read everything together, editing out awkwardnesses of expression, correcting errors, adding new stuff.

(female)

I co-wrote a book with a colleague and really enjoyed the meetings and discussion. I learned a lot from my colleague. We wrote our bits separately and only ever sat at the keyboard together in order to write the introduction. For the most part, though, we divided the topics and met for progress reports.

(female)

I do write with other people. My main collaborator these days is ___ . Our style is for me to write a first draft and then . . . to tinker. I may write notes in the text to him saying things like – 'This is for you to elaborate.' We write separately, then put it together. First of all though, we'll have a detailed – albeit rambling – conversation. ___ and I used to compose together – straight on to paper. I think collaborative writing can allow people to strengthen their writing . . . and I have different strengths in terms of knowledge and perspective. We do share a common mission, though, and we have a similar style. In my experience collaborative writing does not mean that you produce more!

(female)

Finally, collaboration was *not* always seen as a positive and enriching process. I offer a list of potential issues, most of which emerged in the interview data: (1) if the authors possess very different writing styles a collaborative article or book will clearly show the seams and joints; (2) there may be initial disputes about what you're actually agreeing and planning to do, and when to do it by; (3) disagreement can arise about whose names are on a published piece and in which order; (4) there may not be unanimity amongst two or more authors about which journal to send it to, especially if different authors have different motives and are at different career stages; (5) there may not be agreement about what is considered to be *important* to say.

For example:

> Problems? I guess if the co-authors work to very different timescales or with incompatible writing styles then there would be problems.
>   It's hard if the other person wants to take out your 'cherished phrases'. And there may be male/female differences in confidence levels and levels of assertiveness.
>
> (female)

Another person commented on problems when one is seen as 'junior' and the other 'senior', in terms of who does what and which changes are made. It is best to 'decide in advance about things such as your target journal and the order of names, and to work out equal shares and equal division of labour'. She talked of enjoying working with a named person who 'is generous with his writing and whom she can trust' (for further discussion on the benefits and drawbacks of collaboration in writing, see Ashton-Jones, 1997).

People's attitude to writing and the writing process

Attitudes vary:

> I hate it. But then, there's nothing else I'd rather do! A real love–hate relationship. I often feel when I'm having one of those days when I can't even produce a sentence that I can't do it and shouldn't be putting myself through the agony. I rarely read anything I've written, and when I do, sometime after, I often have no recollection of having written it. I sometimes wonder where the words came from. Did I write that?
>
> (female)

> I really enjoy it. I find it difficult, of course, but I do like the process of thinking hard and I also enjoy 'playing with words' a lot. I find it hard to stick to word limits as I always want to explain every detail.
>
> (female)

> I don't enjoy it – partly because I think I am better at some other things, partly because it is a solitary pursuit, partly because it is such hard work!
>
> (male)

> I enjoy getting ideas from writing and I enjoy the satisfaction of a finished 'product'. There's nothing I dislike about it, but I guess I don't like it so much that it takes priority over the rest of work and life – it just fits in. There's something I don't like beforehand, which is the feeling that I don't know if I have anything worth saying about the thing I'm about to write about; it's a sort of 'is it going to be worth it?' feeling. It's sometimes

easy and sometimes a battle. It's just the same writing music, for me and for others. Even for the 'masters' – Beethoven agonized, Brahms rejected some of his early works and had them destroyed, whereas Bach, Haydn, Schubert and Mozart couldn't stop writing – it fell out of them.

(male)

I do enjoy writing, especially when I have quality time to read, write and think. I like it least when I'm rushed. I like it most when I feel very strongly about what I'm writing, which applies to most of the writing I do. The pleasure is about developing thinking through writing and realizing that a point of view is emerging almost as I'm writing – and it wasn't there initially.

(female)

I always enjoy it when it's going well and things start to flow. It doesn't happen that often, but it feels like the writing is almost happening on its own. But at other times it feels like I'm getting in the way of the writing. [She compared the good times with Mozart's metaphor of his acting or being like a 'tube' for his music to flow through.]

(female)

I tend to find it quite a pressured activity. So I guess, to be honest, I don't enjoy it; the reason being that the main barrier for me is time. I tend to get feelings of guilt.

(male)

It's a struggle – what I like most is when it's finished. There's a strange combination of relief and pride.

(female)

It is a struggle, it's a real struggle. You're laying yourself bare: what will people think about it? That can mean that you get completely stuck and not want to write.

(female)

It is often a struggle – but it's the part of the academic role that I like most.

(male)

Aids and barriers

Interviewees were asked about circumstances or things that helped them whilst writing and also about barriers and how they dealt with 'writer's block':

I get it all the time and I don't deal with it. I just stay there and plug away. I have to have total silence else I can't think. I can't write at work because the interruptions are too distracting. There have been times when I give myself rewards – Cadbury's Creme Eggs, a fag (though that's almost twenty years ago now). I do sometimes go and stand in the shower for fifteen minutes or so and I find that can make me feel better.

(female)

If I get stuck, I re-read what I have already produced and often spend a bit of time rephrasing things or clarifying. This usually helps me get in the frame of mind for writing and I can then continue by building on the writing already there. If that is no help I might read for a while and this may give me a few ideas on how to get going or I might draw diagrams. I use the diagrams to set out my ideas in a different way than words and this might then help to clarify what I am trying to do.

(female)

I don't know where to go next. Sometimes I just give up and do something else. Other times I go back to another chapter or a different sub-heading, or even my spidergram. Other times I just try to write my way through it, knowing that I'll probably delete most of it.

(female)

It seems that different people like to work at different times of the day under different conditions and have different routines and avoidance strategies:

I like mostly silence, sequestered from others (I write in the attic of a three-storey house), a view out to the garden, a cat at my feet. Radio 4 in the morning.

(female)

I find procrastination to be a useless but common avoidance strategy. I write (and do most things) best in the morning and would regard 9–1 as being optimum writing time. I tend to leave routine chores (referencing, etc.) for late afternoon.

(male)

Silence (or as near as possible) is great, essential. Good light and somewhere to spread out papers are also good. Background noise and interruptions are barriers. I can go without food and drink when I'm into it. No particular time of day is best for me.

(male)

I need silence, no noise at all. I write at the desk in my study, with the desk cleared of clutter. I write best in the morning between 8 and 1. Around the block or to-the-newsagents walk for ten minutes helps enormously.

(female)

I had a colleague once who said: 'If I don't write in the morning, I can't write all day' . . . and I really relate to that. There can be days on end where I just sort of go back and only move forward a sentence at a time. I find it's best just to leave it and do something else. Often if you do leave it, you find that something happens, out of the blue, that suddenly gives a different perspective on what you were writing about . . . and you can come back and start again. I suppose it's the sub-conscious working on things – it leaves the mind open. [She compared it with meditation, opening up the bigger picture.]

(female)

I'm not an early morning writer. I pad about until about half past ten, moving papers around and looking at books. I suppose I'm working my way into it. All being well I could then do a solid eight hours, give or take the odd bag of crisps, coffee, biscuit or rice cake. I can go on and work quite late, when the world goes dark and quiet. My favourite place is the spare room, which is a complete tip. I can't write in my office. I like to be at home in comfy clothes with no shoes.

(female)

One person (an extremely experienced, widely known author) suggested that he did not accept writer's block, although he did have good days and bad days:

I don't get writer's block because I don't regard writing as an inspirational thing. I work on the premise that it's 90 per cent effort, so I just work my way through it. But I have good days and bad days, when you think 'if I carry on like this it's going to take me ten years to write this paper'. [A good day?] A thousand words is a very good day. I average about 500 words a day.

This writer had almost a ritual that he followed when writing papers or a book:

I start at 8 o'clock in the morning, I work until 1 p.m. So I do five hours with two short coffee breaks. I then have lunch at 1 p.m., but never before; I then fall asleep. I'll wake up, have a cup of tea, then try to do two more hours, but this is mostly reading through and checking. But I couldn't do this more than two or three times a week, even on Sabbatical. I think the most anybody's got in them is five good hours.

Other writing

Of my small but interesting sample, only a few engaged in much 'other writing' of a serious kind, i.e. apart from writing 'shopping lists', e-mails, occasional letters, or 'admin. writing'. Of those who did write for other purposes, some wrote poetry and fiction. One expressed her ambition to write lots of children's books when she retires. One male respondent (an accomplished musician) writes music and finds this very satisfying. Another writes textbooks for major publishers and finds that this has helped his 'academic writing' in developing his skill of 'proofreading and picking up on inconsistencies'. One female respondent talked of the importance of writing her own diary or 'reflective journal':

> I just do it; I don't worry about the audience. It's more about just getting stuff out of your own system. If I'm really puzzled about something I just sit down and write about it for five or six minutes – it doesn't matter what you write, you just see what happens. It's like writing from the inside out. [This process helped to get her re-started on her Ph.D. thesis.]

This issue of the *inhibiting effect* of writing for an audience came up in other interviews and is discussed next.

Open forum

A real ragbag of issues was raised in this section of the interviews. I have tried to categorize them, somewhat arbitrarily. Firstly, the issue of the audience (or at least the writer's constant awareness of an audience), particularly a highly critical peer group, came up several times as a potential inhibitor to the act of writing.

> You're laying yourself bare: what will people think about it? That can mean that you get completely stuck and not want to write. Some audiences in your mind can be less inhibiting than others, such as our Ed.D. students rather than my academic peers. Not that they are a lesser audience, I just think of them as an audience I can engage with, and I know how I want to get things across to those people. Writing an e-mail can be liberating, you can push the boat out . . . you have that liberty to play around with ideas. (It's like a midway thing between speaking and writing.) A 'fallow' period between chunks of writing activity can help too.
>
> (female)

Secondly, related to this, were the additional constraints imposed by external conditions:

We seem to be in an age of constraint – from funding bodies, both public and private, and from the university itself. Even the artificial creation of 'research centres' seems to me to have nothing to do with the kind of writing that I'm interested in and much to do with defining and controlling writing, thereby turning academics into technicians of approved research. That's a pity.

(male)

Another spoke of the way that academics can almost afford to be less constrained in their writing as they become more established and how therefore a person's writing 'changes over time'. He cited research that has shown how 'formality in writing' increases until tenure is secured, and then the temptation is to 'write what you want'. Writing is determined by status.

A third issue that came up was the problematic connection between reading and writing:

The move from doing your reading to doing your writing can be a difficult one. I sometimes start by doing just a piece of 'stream of consciousness' writing, to say 'what do I feel about the issues?' Just to break that *fear* of going from 'all these people have written all these things', where do I start? Reading can be inhibiting: it can take away your confidence to write. Reading different things can toss you around like a cork; sometimes I lose myself, and one of the things I'm still trying to develop is *me* in the writing, still trying to find my own voice. Writing with a word processor has given me more confidence and flexibility. I'm not afraid to delete things I've written and start again.

(female)

Reading is a good way of filling in time and not starting to write. [When should we stop?] When things start to repeat themselves. That gives you a feel for what the 'hooks' are, and at least gives you some key headings for what you're writing. Sometimes I read until I find the hook, really.

(female)

In the open discussion, several people spoke of the importance or indeed the necessity of 'opening up' the whole business of academic writing and of engaging in more discussion of it:

The business of 'doing things academic' is a secret garden that needs opening up. It's partly because all you see are these final, polished bits of writing and you never know what went on behind that. It looks like it just landed there on the page, very cleverly and very magically. [See

Sir Peter Medawar's 1963 paper on this.] Opening up the secret garden would make it easier to write because then you'd be less scared.

(female)

There are tacit rules and principles in academic writing. Learning how to write like that is difficult. That's a learning process that never ends. We don't actually spend enough time talking about those things. The 'academic virtues': Is this well argued? Is it evidence-based? Is it clear? Is it cogent? All those things are the outcome of study, thought, perseverance, reflection, attention to detail . . . all that sort of stuff. We need to be more up front about that. I don't think we're sufficiently self-critical of each other's writing. You do get a lot of 'back-biting' and bitchiness . . . but there's not much honesty and openness going on. We should all be critical friends to each other's work.

(male)

Recurrent themes in these interviews

Several themes recur in the above interview data – I found it quite heartening that many of them relate well to previously published literature on this area (see next section). The main themes seem to be:

  1 Planning is an important activity for all writers. The extent and style of the planning seem to vary, but all plan in some way. Some writers plan in a very visual way by using mind mapping or spidergrams and use metaphors such as sketching the landscape, taking a route or forming a map. Others seem to plan in a more verbal way. There seems to be a 'sub-text' in the responses of some authors, particularly those who do not see themselves as conscientious planners, that planning is a 'good thing' and should be done.

  2 For all these writers, the business of writing is part of their professional identity. It is also an activity which makes them feel part of a community of some kind.

  3 Everyone interviewed writes drafts and redrafts, some to a greater extent than others.

  4 Writing is seen as a learning process by most authors. They talk of learning through their writing, as opposed to writing activity occurring as a result of their learning. Similarly, writing is a form of thinking. Learning and thinking come from writing rather than preceding it. This ties in with several studies reporting that writers see the act of writing as an aid to thinking (e.g. Hartley, 1992b and Wason, 1980).

  5 A wide range of metaphors is used when writers reflect on the writing process. Interviewees talked of icebergs breaking out into open water, of things being lashed together, of plaiting and weaving and of writing 'oozing out'.

6 Fear of exposure and feelings of apprehension are common – in my sample they seem to be more apparent in women, but I would not dare generalize from this number, and anyway my suspicion is that women are more likely to admit to these feelings than men. Self-belief and self-esteem are certainly a vital factor in writing for publishing. There seems to be an extensive literature in this area, based largely on Bandura's writing on self-belief, self-concept or 'self-efficacy' (most recently, Bandura, 1997).

7 Support and collaboration are important to writers. Even when they are not writing collaboratively, people welcome supportive yet critical feedback from friends or colleagues. Yet many still fear unhelpful and over-critical comment from unknown referees. Some important emotions, such as bravery and fear, are involved here. There are also important power relationships, as we see in a later chapter on peer review.

8 The context in which people write and their goals in writing are of key importance. Their reasons for writing and the audience they have in mind determine not only the way they work but also their attitude to it, i.e. the affective side of the process. Some authors are far more work-oriented and utilitarian in their approach than others.

9 Many feel the need for incubation, for lying fallow, or for mulling things over during the business of writing something – especially during a long piece of work such as a book. This may have implications for the way we view the RAE.

Research on the writing and composing process

A substantial amount of work has been done in researching the act of writing. The full range of work cannot be reviewed here, but it is worth devoting some space to the key points, particularly those that relate to the above sample of responses from relatively experienced authors.

Models of writing

Hartley (1992a) provided a valuable review of the research on writing carried out up to that date. He starts from what he terms the 'most influential approach', the model put forward by Hayes and Flower (1986), known as the cognitive process model of writing. The three key elements in their model are:

Planning: this encompasses the wide range of thinking activities – about the content of the text and how it can be organized – that are needed before the writer can put words onto paper.
Translating: this is the physical act of putting the content of the planning process into written words on paper or screen (this has been called transcribing, sometimes composing).

Reviewing: this involves the activity of evaluating what has been written, rethinking, replanning and revising.

Overarching these three elements is the activity of *monitoring*. This is the act of overviewing the writing process and deciding when to switch from one aspect to another, e.g. when one has 'generated enough ideas and is ready to write' (Hayes and Flower, 1986). It seems that skilled writers move continually from one stage of writing to another: e.g. planning may occur throughout composing/translating. However, some researchers (such as Hartley and Knapper, 1984 and Hartley, 1992a) argue that it is useful to separate the three main stages when writing in order to improve one's writing skills. Thus during planning, the broad issues and areas should be mapped out, along with the sequence for them. During the translating stage, the writer should then write as quickly and as freely as possible, even to the extent of ignoring punctuation or rules of grammar (see Elbow, 1981, who calls this 'freewriting'). Revising and editing can follow later.

The model seems to be widely used and accepted. Those who have criticized it have done so if it is seen as a linear process (although Hayes and Flower did not imply that it should be). For example, Humes (1983) reports on her empirical research into 'writing processes and sub-processes', which concludes that writers move back and forth between sub-processes, i.e. the whole process is recursive rather than linear. Thus planning, say, is a thinking process that writers engage with throughout the composing process. Similarly, Elbow (1973 and 1981) criticized the 'classic model' of writing which implies that a linear path occurs from sorting out our meaning, thinking and planning, then actually writing (translating or transcribing), finishing with revising. Elbow says that this idea of writing is 'backwards' (1973: 14). In practice, it is only at the end of the process 'that you know what you want to say and the words you want to say it with'. Elbow uses the metaphors of 'growing and cooking' as a way of viewing writing. He describes the model at length, but in brief it involves firstly getting some ideas 'out onto paper' so that we can interact with them, almost creating a gap between us and the words; this is followed by the cooking process when we allow ideas to interact, talk to people about what we've written and get things to brew and ferment. These metaphors are similar to some of those in my own interviews and relate to the needs of some to chew things over or to lie fallow for a while, and perhaps walk the dog or have a sleep.

The responses from my own interviews show writers on a continuum from linear to recursive in their mode of writing. It seems that the extent to which people pre-plan and perhaps follow a linear process, or in contrast constantly flit from stage to another, does vary widely from one writer to another. Perhaps a person's habits and ground rules for personal writing are established at a relatively early age, but I can only speculate on reasons for differences here.

Skilled writers compared with unskilled

Hayes and Flower (1986) and other researchers since have done extensive work on how much revising different writers do. They suggest that 'experts' revise more than novices. They also revise at a higher level.

More generally, they and other authors have tried to identify the key differences between experienced, skilled writers and those who are less skilled or perhaps novices. The key points from this literature can be summarized (see Hartley, 1992a) as follows:

- Skilled writers revise more than novices. 'Expert' writers (as Hayes and Flower, 1986 call them) attend more to global problems (e.g. resequencing, moving and rewriting large chunks of text) when revising than do novices.
- Skilled writers are better at detecting problems in their text, diagnosing the problems and putting them right. (Generally, however, writers find it harder to see problems in their own writing than they do in others' – hence the importance of a critical friend, as we saw in the interview data.)

Grabe and Kaplan (1996: 240) give their own summary of the practices of good writers, many of which again relate interestingly to my interview data. Some characteristics of 'good writers' are that they:

- Plan for a longer time and more elaborately
- Review and re-assess their plans on a regular basis
- Consider the reader's point of view when planning and composing
- Revise in line with global goals and plans rather than merely editing small, local segments.

Grabe and Kaplan (1996: 118) also, rather cruelly, identify characteristics of 'less skilled writers'. Mainly, they begin to write 'much sooner', with less time taken for initial planning, producing less elaborate 'pre-writing notes'. They do not or cannot make major revisions or undertake major reorganizations of their content and they do not make use of major ideas in their writing which could act as overarching guides for planning, composing and making the piece more coherent (Scardamalia and Bereiter, 1987).

The importance of context and goals

At least one of the interviews above points to the importance of viewing any person's writing in its social and political context. What are the person's motives and goals? What are the conditions (constraints, rewards and pressures) under which they write? In other words, the context is as important as the text. Grabe and Kaplan (1996) summed this up by saying that 'writing should be viewed as a set of practices which are socially contextualised' (p. 17), that 'writing can only be understood from the perspective of a social context and not as a product of a single individual' (p. 94) and that 'writing is a goal-driven activity'.

The goals of the writers mentioned above are determined by the context in which they write, as are their motives, their constraints and the pressures they experience. Some writers appear more utilitarian and goal driven than others, but the common factor is that they all write in an institutional and political context, a regime – and this inevitably shapes how they write and *what they write*. The next chapter examines context more closely by exploring the activity of writing for, and getting published in, refereed journals.

What can we learn from reflecting on the writing process?

One of my respondents talked of the value of 'opening up the secret garden'; another compared the business of writing with sex, in that both are activities that we do in private but don't often talk about. A third talked of being critical friends to each other's writing, which links with the notions of community and professionalism.

I hope that this chapter has at least offered reassurance and insight to those who read it: the writing process is a complex one; it is in some senses a struggle for many people; reflecting on our own writing processes is a valuable activity; it is enjoyable and helpful to share these reflections; there is a range of styles and approaches to planning and composing, but there is no right way of writing. Perhaps it is this last point that needs to be remembered most by those who manage institutions, departments and assessment exercises. Managerial and assessment structures need to recognize the diversity of styles and approaches and allow for these diversities.

Chapter 4

Publishing in journals

The processes involved in writing an article, submitting it to a journal and eventually seeing it published (or not, as the case may be) have sometimes been described as a 'black hole' (Day, 1996). Many of these processes can be and have been examined, but there are still certain elements of mystique, tacit knowledge and less than rational practice involved. The approach taken here is to examine the publishing process and the practices of writing, editing and refereeing from two perspectives: the writer's and the editors' and referees'. If we examine and reflect on these practices, the aim of 'getting published' in a journal can (to some extent) be clarified, eased and assisted.

FROM THE WRITER'S PERSPECTIVE

This part of the chapter examines journal publishing from the writer's perspective: why do it? How should we choose the appropriate journal and aim for it? What kind of responses could we expect, and how should we deal with them?

Journals: what are they and why bother with them?

Writing your article, submitting it to a journal and 'exposing yourself' to unknown referees not only is hard work but can also be daunting and fear-provoking. Why go to all this effort and possible pain?

There are several answers to this. Firstly, by getting your work published in a refereed journal you become 'part of the literature'. Journals act as an archive in a very important, tangible sense. Your work is out there, on paper (usually) and housed safely and publicly in a library (this, incidentally, is one of the criticisms of purely electronic publishing that we discuss later – the work is not archived in the same tangible way, in some eyes). Secondly, your written work has been given some sort of 'stamp of approval' by outsiders (though it may only be two in some cases). It acquires an authority, which a self-published, non-refereed paper does not. Thirdly, as we discuss later in looking at the editorial and peer-review process, it should be the better for it. Many

tors, in my own research interviews and in past literature, have said that ir main aim is to act not so much as gatekeepers but as 'improvers' or facili- rs. This is a positive way for authors to view the submission and refereeing cess: as a way of making their paper better. Fourthly, a published piece d this includes publications in all the forms presented in Chapter 3) is far re likely to be read, to be disseminated and make a contribution than some rt of self-publication.

There is some useful and interesting discussion on this in the literature. Thyer, for example (Thyer, 1994), describes journals as 'archival data sources' (p. 3). He talks of the importance of their 'public accessibility'. Another aspect he discusses at some length is their 'self-correcting nature':

> An article published in a journal is eagerly examined by hoards of jealous peers, each anxious to find mistakes in your work. If such are found, your rivals can submit responses to your article for publication in the journal your work appeared in, and you can prepare rebuttals, all available for present and future researchers to examine. Eventually, it is hoped, truth will emerge from this process.
>
> (1994: 3)

This is perhaps a rather over-stated view, with a slightly traditional notion of 'truth', and inaccurate in that no journal is 'self-correcting' since the correcting can only be done by the people who scrutinize it and take time and trouble to write for it. But one can see what Thyer is getting at. Work published in journals is exposed to scrutiny and laid open to response and rebuttal and the chance for responding to that. The dialogue is continuing and publicly access- ible – and laid down in history or archived. People can look back on debates and exchanges, sometimes heated, which happened decades ago. We can use hindsight to gain a view of the recurring debates that have peaked and troughed like an oscillating wave over a long period. On a shorter timescale, false claims and discoveries, such as the startling claim by Stanley Pons and Martin Fleisch- mann that nuclear fusion could be achieved in a test tube, can be exposed for what they are (in this case, bad science, as told by Close, 1991 in the story of cold fusion).

Choosing the right target

It is worth the effort and the pangs of apprehension that go with subjecting your writing to the much-talked-about 'peer-review process'. So how should we go about it? There is some useful literature on this, but first here is my view. One should always aim carefully at one particular target – not two targets or three, but one. The first, and probably the biggest and most important, job is to decide which one.

Weighing up the pecking order

One of the first decisions, especially if you are working in a field such as education where there are a huge number of journals, is to decide how 'high' you should aim. In discussion, and in the literature, people often present the choice in the following way. On the one hand, you may wish to have your work published in the most prestigious, well-regarded and widely read journals and score what many people (not me) call 'Brownie points', especially for the RAE. On the other, you may be more of a pragmatist who goes for those lower in the hierarchy in the hope that their standards are more lenient, the rejection rate is lower and there is not a time lag of two years between submission and publication. This decision is also bound up with the question of who we are writing for: teachers and other practitioners, or academics and researchers?

There may well be some truth in this portrayal of a hierarchy of journals. I often think that way myself. But we should also beware of the underlying assumptions and dangers. Firstly, on what grounds can we be clear about the pecking order or hierarchy? Also, can we assume that all of the most 'prestigious' journals do have higher rejection rates than those 'below' them? Similarly, can we assume that the less prestigious are more likely to referee your article quickly and get it into print efficiently and without delay?

The likely time lag between submitting your article and seeing it in print (even in the unlikely event that it is accepted without any amendment) is an important criterion in choosing the right journal, and authors are well advised to do their best to find this out (if they can). Again, we cannot assume that the less prestigious journals are the quickest to publish.

Assessing prestige, impact and status

Can numerical assessments be made of status, prestige or impact? In 2002, a website was available that allegedly calculated the 'Prestige Factor' (PF) of a journal. The site, which for some reason unknown to me is now defunct (it was located at www.prestigefactor.com), ranked nearly 1,500 social science journals, giving them a 'PF' which took into account six independent variables, and was said to assess the 'true value' of a journal.

To my knowledge, there has been no similar, publicly available attempt to rank and quantify the 'prestige' or status of journals. The *Social Sciences Citation Index* (SSCI) includes an assessment of the impact factor, based on the number of citations made. It also includes a measure of the 'immediacy factor' of a journal, i.e. the time lapse between the publication of a journal and citations of articles from it, and 'citation half life', a measure of the length of time over which a publication is cited. Many groups consider the SSCI to be an important and influential database in considering status. Certainly, it provides useful measures of citation and impact. But the processes or means by which a journal

comes to be included in the list of 1,725 titles forming the SSCI are not necessarily related to status. For example, of the 700 or more education journals only
around 90 are listed in the database, and the criteria by which this sub-set is
included are by no means clear. Cause and effect are somewhat cloudy here –
inclusion in the SSCI may raise status, but status does not seem to be the
major prerequisite for entry to it.

Personally, I don't find numerical indices convincing. So in writing this book,
I decided to ask a range of journal editors for their view on what counts as an
'eminent, high-status academic journal'. The response from some was a verbal
version of a shrug of the shoulders, as if to say: 'well, we know one when we
see one'. Others were prepared to expand, even though elements of the response
were slightly circular and tautologous:

> Yes, clearly there is a pecking order amongst journals. The criteria are
> numerous, but the main ones, I think, are the extent to which a journal
> is perceived by the research community as, in some way or another,
> 'eminent'; and the extent to which it has a wide international audience.
> The other main criterion, I think, is the extent to which the journal is
> the 'journal of first resort' for a large number of people. Another, related
> to that, is the rejection rate of a journal. Generally, the more prestigious
> and eminent journals have the highest rejection rates, and are therefore
> the most difficult to get into.

Others felt clear that in their own domain there is a hierarchy:

> There is a pecking order in the field of literacy. Journals *high* in the order
> are those that reach a wide audience and are known to publish papers of
> a high quality. It's more about the journals we read and use than a citations
> index, for example.

Another felt that there are two hierarchies in journals, professional and
academic:

> Journal _____ is high in the order for professional journals, but not
> academic.

> Who writes for it? Who gets published in it? Are they the famous names in
> a field?

One editor reported that his journal did not have a 'pre-RAE glut' of submissions from the UK, and this suggests that 'at least in the UK it is not
regarded as particularly high status because we didn't get a rush of contributions'. He described his journal as:

general and eclectic; higher-status journals tend to be more specific and focused, in a particular field. I think people will submit to them first, before us. Incidentally, I'm not sure that it's harder to get into high-status journals than others. In my experience, I've had to make fewer revisions for the higher-status ones.

The people involved in a journal were deemed to be the key factor by one editor:

Who's editing it, and who's on the editorial board?

In summary, there seems to be a range of factors by which people judge the status of a journal: is it widely read and subscribed to? Who publishes it? Who publishes *in it*? Is it international? Is it the journal of first resort? Does it have a glut of 'pre-RAE submissions'? Does it have a high rejection rate? Does it have a strong and wide intellectual base? None of these criteria is non-problematic.

Aiming for the target: the groundwork

After you have decided on the level to aim at, a lot more work needs to be done before you decide on the right target, let alone submit your paper to it.

The first question must be: which journal is your subject matter, and your treatment of it, 'right' for? Many submitted articles do not even reach referees because they are deemed inappropriate for the journal or they don't match the journal's objectives (see editors' interviews below). The first job is to decide who you are writing for – for example, are you aiming at practitioners, researchers, academics, policy makers or some combination of them? Next, it makes sense to get to know the whole range of possible outlets for one's work. Consult directories such as Ulrich's; scan journals on library shelves; search electronically; see where the 'respected authors are publishing' (Day, 1996); ask colleagues – what do they read and where do they publish? Then, it is necessary to go deeper (Day, 1996). Read the journals, on paper or on screen. Examine the contents lists and study the back issues. Who are the authors? Who are their audiences? What have been the recurring themes and debates?

Above all, and every editor will emphasize this, scrutinize the notes for authors published in the journal itself and usually on their website too. Some (not all) also publish criteria by which articles are judged and refereed. Do check the website. Box 4.1 shows two examples that make their aims, policy and scope perfectly clear.

Finally, read past articles in the back issues; read the editorials, looking for the themes, aims, perspectives and direction of the journal; study the make-up of the editorial board and the referees (if they are listed).

Box 4.1 Examples of journal policy statements and instructions for authors

---

1   *Journal of Education for Teaching*
    Publishing Policy
    The *Journal of Education for Teaching* publishes original contributions
    on the subject of teacher education in its widest sense: initial prepara-
    tion, further professional education and staff development. Contri-
    butions may comprise scholarly discussion of new issues, reports of
    research, reviews of research in particular fields, reports of develop-
    ments and contributions to debate on teacher education generally or
    on specific issues. Short statements concerning research in progress
    (normally up to 300 words) are invited for *JET*'s 'Research Notice-
    board'. Short accounts of innovatory practice (normally up to 600
    words) are invited for the *JET* 'In Practice' section. Rejoinders to
    articles are welcome as a contribution to debate among teacher
    educators.

2   *Gender and Education*
    Instructions for Authors
    Contributors should bear in mind that they are addressing an inter-
    national audience. The Editors welcome a variety of contributions
    that focus on gender as a category of analysis in education and that
    further feminist knowledge, theory, consciousness, action and debate.
    Education will be interpreted in a broad sense to cover both formal
    and informal aspects, including nursery, primary and secondary educa-
    tion; youth cultures inside and outside schools; adult, community,
    further and higher education; vocational education and training;
    media education; parental education. Contributors are asked to avoid
    unnecessary or mystifying jargon and to use non-sexist and non-racist
    language.

In short, an author needs to know, or at least have some feel for, the *ground
rules* of a journal before writing for it. Some of these may be explicit and
stated in writing; others may be implicit and will need to be discerned rather
than read from a website or a back cover.

Bazerman (1983: 160) put it this way, in a rather old-fashioned style:

> the writer must know the problems of the field, the ideals and ethos of the
> field, the accepted justificatory arguments, the institutional structure in
> which the knowledge is to be communicated and the criteria of adequacy
> by which the innovative work will be judged.

Grabe and Kaplan (1996: 171) highlight a 'complex set' of five skills that authors need in getting published. I have adapted them and summarized them as follows:

1   A sense of appropriateness and scope: authors need a 'sophisticated sense' of appropriate areas of research, of proper research questions and of acceptable research designs.
2   A sense of context: a cognizance of 'intertextuality', i.e. a clear sense of what others have already said on the topic and of how to incorporate that into one's own writing.
3   Alignment: the skill of aligning one's own work with the recognized leadership in the field, so that 'the leadership will seem to legitimise their work'.
4   A sense of audience: being aware of what will influence the referees/peer reviewers and the general readership in that journal or discipline.
5   A sense of style or genre: as Grabe and Kaplan put it, though not in the clearest of English, the skill of conveying 'the necessary rhetorically charged information through appropriate mechanisms of persuasion within the constraints of a formal objective format'.

After all this groundwork, it may well be worth a 'sounding out' letter to the editor, outlining your article in a very short synopsis and asking if it will be appropriate.

Writing and targeting

My own view is that you need to have a specific journal in mind *before* starting to write the actual article (not before you start doing any writing at all, though). Then, write the paper with that particular journal in mind. This may sound a very instrumental approach – it also suffers from the drawback that if the specific targeted journal rejects your article then more work is involved in adapting it for a new target. But in my opinion, the opposite approach is just not tenable – i.e. writing an article of unspecified length, style and format and then thinking about how to shape it for a particular journal's rules, track record, history and implicit or explicit requirements.

After you have chosen a target journal, several rules are worth following when writing. Henson (1999) gives some useful 'handy hints':

•   Read recent issues and shape your article accordingly
•   Look for traits/characteristics in the journal and attempt to use them as a model
•   Keep to the word length
•   Follow the journal's guidelines to authors with care
•   Try to make a 'unique contribution', however small.

Henson (1999) also gives a list of common mistakes made by people when writing for journals: lack of familiarity with the journal and its aims and content; wrong style; wrong formatting; wrong length; poor presentation, e.g. grammatical and typing errors; no substance ('much ado about nothing'); unreadability; failure to check your typescript (or have a critical friend check it) before sending it off.

In his excellent book on writing, Woods (1999: 115–118) gives some interesting and practical advice on targeting journals. He tells how he submitted a paper to one journal and (after a six-month wait) was told in a curt letter that it was not considered 'suitable', despite the fact that he was on the journal's reviewing panel. He then sent it to another journal (American based); he was not quite sure about its ground rules or its 'discourse'. They wrote back asking for a very condensed version for their report section. He was not happy about doing this, so sent it to a third journal, which accepted it 'within a matter of weeks'. The moral that he draws from his own story is that he would have saved a lot of time and trouble if he had 'studied the suitability of the journals in the first place'.

Woods (1999: 118) also talks of the importance of developing some 'contingency plans' for a journal article so that 'all is not wasted' if one's article is rejected by its first target: 'If you are convinced that you have a quality product you should leave no stone unturned.' Persevere.

I leave the last word on this issue to an author writing over fifty years ago on the preparation of medical papers for publication who concludes, in rather 1950s language:

> If you are sure that you really have observations or ideas which should be published, select your journal carefully with a view to attracting the right type of reader. Then proceed to write your paper to conform to that journal's scope and style. Failure to observe this simple precaution will certainly mean a rejection slip. How are your observations and ideas to be presented?
>
> (Bett, 1952: 13)

The waiting period

Once the journal has been selected and the article and covering letter have been sent, there is no choice but to wait. For how long? What range of responses can one expect? How should one deal with criticism, requests for amendment, or even outright rejection? What goes on in the period between submission and the feedback that an author receives? We consider these issues in the next three sections.

A good journal will notify you and thank you for receipt of your article – an inefficient one may not. You will then have to wait. Some journals (rightly, in my view) have a policy of not keeping authors in suspense for longer than a certain time (six weeks in one case at least). This policy seems humane and professional. Other journals, which are either less efficient or very lax with their team of reviewers, may keep authors waiting for many weeks or even months. In November 2001, I submitted an article to a reputable education journal, which I felt I had carefully targeted. At first I had no acknowledgement after a few weeks that it had arrived, so I asked them by e-mail – it had arrived safely as hard copy in the post. By the end of March 2002, I still had not received feedback from referees, despite politely asking them at the start of that month what the situation was. I politely asked them again (by e-mail) in June 2002 if I could have reviewers' comments. Finally, on 6 July, I received a letter informing me that the article was not considered appropriate for that journal, and advising me to 'submit [my] article elsewhere'. This response had taken eight months. I promptly rewrote and reformatted the article for a different journal and sent it off. They acknowledged its receipt by return of post. In my opinion, the delay created by the inefficiency of the first journal is unacceptable (it is also one of the factors that puts people off publishing, as we saw in Chapter 1). If referees are too busy (or cannot carve out the time in a six-month period) to review papers, then the journal should look for new ones.

Most editors would say that a polite letter or e-mail from an author after a period of about 6–8 weeks inquiring about the current situation would be acceptable. It is then up to the editor to decide how to cajole, chivvy or persuade the reviewers so that the peer-review process can go ahead.

Dealing with a journal's response to your submission

A journal is likely to respond in one of four ways:

1 The article may be accepted as it stands (this is unlikely and uncommon, but it happens).
2 The article may be rejected; sometimes there is a recommendation that you submit it to another journal, often because it is not deemed suitable or appropriate. In some cases, there may simply be a rejection.
3 Minor revisions may be mentioned: often this may be a strong suggestion, or just a hint, that if minor amendments are made (as outlined by one or more referees), then the article will be accepted.
4 Major, more serious revisions may be said to be needed, but again there is often encouragement to make these and resubmit.

The fourth response is a common one, and authors should gear themselves up to expect it. My suggested path to follow, based on my own experience and what editors and other authors have said to me, is as follows:

- Don't take offence.
- Take a short time to get over the blow, whilst perhaps eating some humble pie.
- Carefully study the reviewers' comments one by one and address each one. Revise accordingly. With some you will make significant changes, but with others you may want to stand your ground, provided you have a good reason for doing so (other than being precious).
- Resubmit, explaining in an accompanying letter exactly (one by one) how you have responded to referees' comments, what you have changed and what you have *not* changed, and why.

The response after a resubmission may still be one of the four above. Some journals will require further changes or may be dissatisfied with those you have made. Persevere.

If outright rejection occurs, then (as said above and in the editors' interviews later) it is often due to the unsuitability of the journal anyway. Vent your anger, persevere and find another journal. As Smaby *et al.* (1999) put it:

> If an editor has just rejected your manuscript because it was deemed inappropriate for that particular journal you may feel defeated, humiliated and angry and vow never to write again. Give yourself a few days for 'cooling-off' and then assess your attitude and feelings about having your manuscript rejected.

Smaby *et al.* suggest that the writer then designs a plan and sets up a programme for the next step. They suggest that you leave the typescript for a few days, then look carefully at the editor's letter and the referees' comments again (slowly and coolly). Then go back to researching other possible journals and choose a new target. Revise the article and resubmit. Smaby's research (see later) showed that resubmitted typescripts have a far higher chance of acceptance than first submissions. Perseverance is the key.

One of the editors I interviewed told me that the best advice one could give to a new author would be:

> If you have a paper rejected, you're not the only one. Learn from it; work on the criticisms. Reflect on the criticisms and resubmit. Don't lose heart; don't get depressed.

Another said, in a similar vein, that on receiving referees' comments

> Authors can come back and say 'I totally disagree with this point the referee is making and therefore I do not want to make this change, and

here are the reasons *why*.' A lot of times, young writers don't know that they can make this case to the editor. They can go into negotiation mode.

Reasons for acceptance and rejection: what can past research tell us?

Noble (1989) made a study of twenty-three education journals from five countries, eliciting their grounds for acceptance or rejection. One positive comment was that 'immediate appeal' seemed to be important, i.e. the professional appearance of a typescript, an interesting title and the fact that an author had followed the journal's guidelines. In contrast, reasons for immediate rejection were 'superficial treatment of a subject', not following journal guidelines and 'poor writing'. Other common causes were inappropriateness for the journal and 'trivial work'. From his sample of editors came several key suggestions for authors: write clearly, logically and sequentially; follow guidelines; have the typescript critiqued before submission; aim for clarity, coherence and thoroughness of argument.

Noble's study was an interesting one, although the use of a questionnaire may have restricted the extent to which he was able to probe the replies more deeply and go beyond the superficial. It may also be true that styles of writing, accepted presentation and criteria of quality have changed since 1989.

Smaby *et al.* (1999) carried out an analysis of all 180 scripts submitted to a journal over a period of one year. From a statistical analysis they identified a number of specific factors or characteristics which correlated well with a typescript being accepted for publication. They included the quality of the introduction; the choice of research design and procedures; the presentation and discussion of results; the account of the implications of the work; the use of an appropriate writing style and presentation of the script, including grammar and punctuation; and a collection of factors which can be summed up as the use of 'existing research as a rationale for the research undertaken' (p. 233).

My own interviews with twelve editors, reported in the second part of this chapter, reinforce some of the above, and include several others.

What critical comments can authors expect from referees?

Before we turn to the editors' and referees' perspectives, it may be interesting and perhaps reassuring to read a small sample of critical comments received from journal referees. Some I have received myself; some have been given to me by colleagues. The only alterations made to these extracts from letters are those needed to preserve anonymity.

Encouragement to revise: two categories

I have now heard from the referees who have been reading the article you submitted to this Journal in January, and I am pleased to be able to tell you that they are enthusiastic that we should publish a revised version in a forthcoming issue of ____. They agree that this is an interesting article which deals with an important issue of relevance to our readers. However, they also make a number of points which I should like you to take into account when revising. [The letter then went on to explain five points in detail, including the need to change the title of the paper.]

I am writing to say that unfortunately the Editorial Board and our referees do not recommend publication in its present form of your paper: ____. I attach a summary of their comments and hope you will find them helpful if you wish to revise the paper. If you do wish to revisit the paper with these points in mind we shall be pleased to consider a resubmission. Please note that this would not in any way guarantee publication as your resubmitted paper would again be subject to our refereeing process. [A three-page summary of referees' comments then followed.]

Polite rejections

Thank you very much for sending your paper: ____ for possible publication in ____. The paper has now been reviewed by three senior scholars in the field, whose reports are enclosed. Unfortunately I have to inform you that the paper is unacceptable for publication in the journal. The reviewers all agree that your topic is important, but they also believe that your treatment, specifically the survey structure and analysis, has serious flaws; and even if these are rectified, the reviewers doubt whether the findings warrant publication. Regretfully, I have to say that I concur with their judgement.

I have now received back the referees' reports on your article ____. While they both believe that the article certainly addresses a topic of current concern in relation to the curriculum, they also feel that it needs to address important aspects which are neglected here, such as greater clarity about methodology; case study description in relation to implementation issues; a strengthening of the comment on sectors; more systematic treatment of impact, and a wider sweep in discussion of the discourse. Given these reservations, I regret to have to tell you that I have decided not to publish on this occasion. I hope that this is not too disappointing, and wish you every success in finding a suitable outlet for your article.

I enjoyed reading this paper as it tells a tale with which many of us are only too familiar. And of course, this is one of the main problems with the paper much of what is contained is already well rehearsed and in the public domain. The other major criticism which I have to offer is that ____ is an international journal and this paper contains far too much which excludes an international audience. The writer presumes a great deal of in-depth familiarity on the part of the reader. Regretfully I must suggest that this paper be rejected by ____ for the above reasons.

And, on the same article, but from a different referee:

This is a useful paper – it covers a great deal – perhaps too much. However, it is not suitable for ____ as the policy analysis is somewhat superficial. Also the paper is not user-friendly for an international audience.

A less polite rejection

This is a simplistic and somewhat tendentious descriptive account of some events in over the past 40 years but there is very little attempt to get underneath them and consider what was really going on. My advice, therefore, I am afraid is a firm rejection. These are some of the main reasons. There is no original material. The paper consists of almost random extracts from various authors, mainly their conclusions with little indication of how they arrived at them. In general policy is presented as a series of events, that occur sometimes as a result of government perversity, but otherwise there is no attempt to consider why they happened.

The best source of real referees' comments of which I know is Woods (1999: 121–127). He provides seven pages of critical comments made on journal submissions. The criticisms are of the following: inadequate methods or explanation of them; limited data or misused data; inadequate theory; wrong journal; poor presentation and style; unacknowledged bias; limited analysis and discussion; and finally, dubious ethics. For a humorous and very reassuring account of 'rotten rejections', you might like to read Bernard's book (1990).

Finally, it is worth noting that referees do not always agree. Fiske and Fogg (1990) report a study of 402 reviews of 153 papers submitted to 12 editors of journals in the USA. Frequently, reviewers disagreed, and with those who were highly critical it was often the case that 'two reviews of the same paper had no critical point in common'. Their findings in 1990 resonate with the comments made by editors during my own interview study, which is reported in the next section of this chapter.

FROM THE EDITORS' AND REFEREES' PERSPECTIVES

Editors, working with their referees, can give a paper its official licence to print: the imprimatur. This section of the chapter looks in detail at the editing, refereeing and peer-review processes: how does peer review work? What is good and bad about peer review? How can it be improved? What is the role of the editor? How do editors see themselves? What criteria are used in judging the quality of submitted papers, explicitly and tacitly?

Some of this section is based on past studies of these activities, but the bulk of it draws upon in-depth interviews conducted face to face with twelve editors of well-known journals in the UK. Each interview lasted for between forty-five minutes and an hour and yielded a large amount of qualitative data. The voices and extracts included here are a selection from those interview data.

Why do we subject people to peer review?

This is an area of publishing that has been the focus of a lot of attention and literature over a number of decades. Peer review is a process nearly three centuries old (Zuckerman and Merton, 1971). A fair amount of research has been done on the process in the last twenty years (see, for example, articles ranging from Smith and Gough, 1984 to Brewer *et al.*, 2001). I will briefly consider some of these studies, and later I report on my own interviews with editors.

Bakanic *et al.* (1987) made a huge study of 2,337 typescripts submitted to the *American Sociological Review* over a four-year period. Their results are worth reading in full, but here I give the main points of relevance to this chapter. Firstly, they found that disagreement amongst referees is common. Complete agreement between two referees is rare, about one case in five. Split decisions are therefore the norm (see my data on the editor's role later). Two interesting factors were found that seem to determine the success of a submission: those who referee for a journal are more likely to get published in it; and the prestige of the submitting author's employing institution had a significant positive effect on the success of the paper. This may well be due to the better working environment in a 'prestigious institution', better resources, an ethos that encourages publication and the time provided by the institution for staff to engage in scholarly work. The former factor (being on the reviewing panel) may well be due to some of the factors discussed earlier in this chapter, i.e. knowing how to write for that journal, knowing its ground rules and knowing how to aim at the 'target'. Finally, Bakanic *et al.*'s work tallies with other research in showing that resubmissions have a much greater probability of eventual publication than first submissions. Persevere. Their article concludes with a generally favourable view of the peer-review process, arguing that it 'helps in the construction of scholarship' in a field.

Critics of peer review

Not everyone is as supportive of the concept and practice of peer review. Some view it as highly problematic and suspect. I have heard several voices, in seminars and meetings, who describe the process in different ways: as essentially conservative, preserving existing norms and networks, 'a closed shop', serving in a gatekeeping or policing capacity, keeping people out rather than including them, developing sterility and conformity in scholarly work, unnecessary censorship, or simply unfair and exclusive. These have often been people who have felt the pain of the peer-review process, but they also include others who have published successfully in peer-reviewed journals. Some critics have even voiced the view that electronic journals could create a process by which everything submitted to them would be published, without judgement by others. It would then be the reader's responsibility to decide or judge what should be read, rather than an editorial board which has censored the material in advance, allegedly for the reader's benefit.

There is some support (though not a lot, as one would expect) for these views in the refereed literature. In 1982, Peters and Ceci carried out a controversial and, to some, unethical study, sub-titled 'The fate of published articles submitted again'. Thirteen articles by US authors from 'high-status' institutions, which had been published in reputable psychological journals, were resubmitted, in disguised form, to exactly those journals that had originally published them. Fictitious names and institutions were given in the new covering letters. Only three were spotted as being resubmissions and were therefore rejected, while nine were rejected on other grounds. Only one article was accepted for publication. In the rejections, the most commonly mentioned weakness was 'serious methodological flaws'.

The authors' conclusions are as contentious as their methods. Peters and Ceci suggest that the second group of reviewers may be less competent than the first, or that there was a clear bias towards submissions from authors based in 'high-status' institutions.

The study also seems to point to reviewer unreliability. The authors' own views are made clear, although their value judgements expressed here certainly do not follow from their empirical study:

> Anonymous peer reviews may be more costly than beneficial. A system that could allow a reviewer to say unreasonable, insulting, irrelevant and misinformed things about you and your work hardly seems equitable.
>
> (Peters and Ceci, 1982: 194)

More recent literature on this area has included several important critiques of the notion and the practice of 'peer review'. Lather (1999), writing from what she calls a poststructuralist feminist perspective, talks of how 'practices often viewed as neutral in effect police, produce and constitute a field'. Apple (1999), writing in the same journal, talks of the 'power/knowledge nexus underlying any construction of a field of knowledge and knowing' (citing Popkewitz and Brennan's 1998 book on Foucault). Similarly, Osborne and Brady (2002) talk of the 'power differential' at work in peer reviews:

> Peer review places enormous power in the hands of someone who has contemplated for an hour what the author has contemplated for months.
> (p. 165)

These authors use terms such as 'sleazy', 'secret', 'done behind their backs' and 'closed' in discussing peer review. They advocate a move from a system that is judgemental, destructive, distant, deconstructive and detached to a more caring, sympathetic, constructive, formative and creative climate.

In the same journal, Tobin (2002) stresses the need for induction, mentoring and apprenticeship of new referees, working with more experienced reviewers. However, my own view is that this mentoring process alone is not likely to create the more sympathetic and formative refereeing that is being sought – apprentices and mentees can simply become initiated into existing practices, as happens in other fields.

Larochelle and Desautels (2002) make similar points to those of Apple and others by using a football analogy. They talk of the 'referee regime' that helps to define and enforce the rules of the game, controls movement, and decides who comes onto the field (and who stays on it, I would add). Again, they cite the work of Foucault.

Roth (2002) writes of editorial power and authorial suffering, suggesting that editors exert power while authors often comply, in order to get published. Roth argues that the guiding values in refereeing should be civility and solidarity, rather than the exercise of editorial power.

Reviewer anonymity: benefits and drawbacks?

It is now more or less accepted practice that the reviewer will not be told the name of the author and vice versa (see my own interview data). There has been some discussion over the years of the merits of masked reviewing. Some people feel that referees might be more civil and constructive if their names were declared to the author. Others feel that referees would be less honest, objective and forthright if this were the case. One extensive study of 300 editors and reviewers was conducted in the psychology field in 1993 (Bornstein, 1993). One of the main reasons given by respondents for keeping anonymity was the fear that authors might 'retaliate' against them for criticizing their papers. The main reason given for openness, i.e. revealing reviewers' names, was that the reviewers would become more *accountable* for the assertions they make in their comments. A minority felt that 'bad or abusive' or 'scathing' reviews would be less frequent. However, Bornstein's conclusion was that the majority of editors and referees are 'not enthusiastic' about an open review system – the article concludes, as one would expect, that more research is needed on this area!

As for author anonymity, the debate is still open. Most would argue that authors should always be masked – if not, their name and track record might prejudice the referee, sometimes favourably ('Unto every one that hath shall be given'), sometimes not. Others feel that the author's name should be revealed, as this is part of the process and will give the referees guidance on how they should judge the paper and feedback. In practice, as one of my editor interviewees said, it takes the reviewer all of twenty seconds to work out who the author is.

On humaneness and civility in reviewing

The study cited above (Bornstein, 1993: 370) included several open-ended comments about the review-process. One sensitive reviewer said that 'scathing reviews received by a young author have all the characteristics of a terrorist act – they are quick, seemingly targeted at random and devastating'. Another felt that 'adequate training of reviewers would help'. A third argued that openness is needed because, as a matter of principle, a reviewer would not say anything about an author's paper that he would not 'be willing to say to an author face to face'.

Several authors, and indeed the editors I interviewed, firmly believe that refereeing should be a humane process. One excellent American article, published on the Internet (Sternberg, accessed 25 February 2002), argues persuasively that 'savage reviews are harmful to all concerned' for several reasons: they are unbalanced by failing to point out the positive aspects present in every submission; they 'stretch the truth' by exaggerating the weaknesses of a paper; they create animosity rather than 'collegial interchange'; and perhaps most importantly they undermine the writer's self-belief (Sternberg calls this one's 'self-efficacy': cf. Bandura, 1997). Experienced writers may be able to take savage reviews in their stride. They often have tenure, so their future employment is not at stake. But new authors are often 'taken aback'; they become discouraged and despondent. As Sternberg puts it, the person submitting 'does not yet realise that the problem is in the reviewer, not the material he or she reviewed. The material may in fact be in need of considerable work, but even if it is, there is no need to savagely attack it.' He concludes by arguing that referees 'should not write them' (savage reviews) and editors should not disseminate them. Authors receiving them from a journal should try to ignore the 'ad hominem content and hostile tone' and try to make maximum use of the substantive points made by the referee.

A summary of criticisms of the peer-review process

In summarizing this section of the chapter, I have distilled a total of eleven criticisms (many of which overlap) that can be made of the process of peer review. Many are answered and countered by the comments made by editors in a later section of this chapter. Others are actually reinforced by the same editors:

1   There is a lack of serious attention and quality time invested by reviewers, who often squeeze the job in amongst all their other commitments.
2   There is a lack of agreement on what counts as 'merit' or quality and the criteria used to judge it; and a lack of consistency in applying these criteria, even if they are made explicit. All referees have their own tacit criteria, views, prejudices and agendas.
3   Partiality is shown by editors and referees, especially when they know (or guess) the identity of the author. Anonymity is rarely realized in practice, especially in a small field.
4   The range of peers to which an author's submission may be exposed is narrow, e.g. 'old white men', a term used by Eisenhart (2002).
5   Peers are often 'higher status' than authors, e.g. from more prestigious institutions, older, more accomplished.
6   Editorial judgements of acceptance or rejection are naturally subjective and are based on samples of two, three or at most four opinions.
7   Good researchers and writers are not always good reviewers, and often have no training, induction or mentoring.
8   Peer review has a tendency to uphold conventional, conservative standards and discourage risk taking, innovation and diverse perspectives; journals have a tendency to accept articles which 'fit in'. Peer review is biased in favour of the establishment. It creates a sterile, safe academic world, stifling creativity, originality and difference.
9   Peer review is more akin to censorship than to quality control and quality assurance.
10 Peer review usually consists of a monologue: a one-way statement from referee to an author, rather than a constructive dialogue between them.
11 Peer review slows the whole publication process down, creating a huge time lag between submission and publication.

The editor's perspective

Twelve editors of education journals were interviewed using the schedule shown in Appendix 2 as the main focus. However, many editors deviated from it with interesting expansions and asides. All the interviews were transcribed from tape. The summary below is a distillation of the data, structured roughly along the lines of the interview schedule.

The journals themselves

Some of the journals have been established for over thirty years, including one ('the professional journal') which had just celebrated its 300th edition, while some are newer and one was in its first year of publication. The number of readers in each case is hard to quantify, but one journal claimed to have a print subscription of about 1,000, another claimed 400 subscriptions across 34 countries and another estimated the total of its subscribers as between 500 and 600. One checked the exact figure, which turned out to be 233 (185 from libraries).

Rejections and rejection rates

It was hard to establish a clear figure for rejection rates from each journal. One admitted that 'it is not closely monitored', and this might be typical. One editor estimated a rate of about 30 per cent, while two suggested that theirs was around 80 per cent. This included the newly launched journal who argued that their rejection rate is high because they are a new journal. As one interviewee pointed out, there are two types of rejection, hence the difficulty in quantifying exactly. The first is outright rejection, but more commonly authors are asked to resubmit with 'major amendments'. Many authors do not persevere (even some who are asked to make 'minor amendments'), and this leads to a category that one editor called 'author self-rejection', often from inexperienced authors who are not used to the 'shock', 'blow to their pride', or 'emotional setback' that comes with referees' comments.

Another estimated that:

> I guess we publish eventually around about half of those we receive. But almost none of those are in a recognizable form compared with the original sent in. They go through, usually, two or three rewrites in the mean time. And that's what makes all the difference in the papers.

One editor said that 'nothing ever goes through without at least minor revisions. The majority are graded as "Reject with an invitation to resubmit".'

One point made by all editors is that articles are often rejected, not because of poor quality, but for lack of suitability or appropriateness for the journal.

Becoming an editor

The path to becoming an editor is interesting and perhaps contentious. The process seems to vary enormously, from a route involving personal contacts and grapevines, to the process of 'working your way up', to (in one case only) the post being advertised nationally and the editor applying successfully for it. In some cases, the publishers of the journal may be asked to suggest a new editor. One editor talked of having his 'arm twisted'. Another talked of serving on the editorial board, then being asked to take over as editor and having this approved by the society covering the field of study of the journal. One was, in a sense, passed the baton: 'I was appointed by the outgoing editor and served a twelve-month apprenticeship.' The editor of the new journal talked of 'conceiving and initiating the journal after seeing a clear gap in the field'. Others were involved through their professional connections, and they formed a team of five. In another case, a group of four people formed the journal from a previous one and 'decided amongst themselves that he would become editor'. He had been an editor for eleven years ('they just keep asking me to carry on'). Another had been associate editor at first, and then 'they needed to bring on a new pair of hands'.

Another became editor because:

> The idea behind the journal was partly my own. It became 'assumed' that I would take the idea through. I formed a working group and wrote a proposal that was revised and rewritten, then sent to various publishing houses. I did all the work, so there was a kind of inevitability about my becoming editor. The working group 'approved' of me, and I'm still accountable to them, now called the executive group. So I don't have complete freedom, even down to the kinds of letters I send to referees and authors.

Finally, with another relatively new journal, people from the editorial board were asked to apply for the editorship. Two did, their applications were discussed by the rest of the board and they were asked to be joint editors.

The editor's role

From the interviews it emerged that the editors see themselves as performing a range of different roles – some emphasized certain aspects of their role more than others.

The filter

Some editors do see themselves as the initial or preliminary filter on articles submitted, although (as we see later) few would admit to being gatekeepers:

> I am the preliminary filter. I make a preliminary judgement on whether submitted papers are of sufficient quality to go to external referees. I also communicate the outcome of that refereeing process to the authors.

> I filter papers as they come in [some are not even sent out to referees].

Another talked of avoiding 'troubling' the referees:

I would scan them first of all, to make sure that they're worth troubling reviewers with.

Similarly:

> A manuscript arrives and I read it on arrival, in order to judge whether it fits in with the journal's policy. If it does not, I return it immediately to the author, because I'm not inclined to use up valuable referees' time. So I do screen. If I get an article that radically exceeds our word limit, it goes straight back to the author.

> I think the editor needs to be very hands-on. The editor needs to be a gate-keeper, dealing with the preliminary filtering. I look for the relevancy of the question, to see if the literature review is up-to-date, in particular to see if the person has tapped into a topic we've been dealing with in the journal pages. When you think about it, it doesn't make sense to send something into the pipeline of review that's going to take 6, 8, 12 weeks to come out the other end, knowing that it's going to get a 'Reject'. There's no sense in leading someone on. I can feed back to the author within a few days: 'this isn't the right journal' or 'you might like to take it to a different audience'.

One described this initial role as a 'screening process: does it fit the aims and scope of the journal? Has the author read the guidance notes?'

> An awful lot of contributors don't read our guidelines, or just skim them quickly – even established authors who should know better, even eminent professors. It does irritate me. If the rules can be obeyed by a research associate, they can be obeyed by a professor.

This initial filtering phase is asymmetrical in a sense, since editors can say 'no' to articles but they cannot say 'yes'.

All editors said that they are happy to deal with letters of inquiry or solicitations of the kind 'I've written a paper on this topic: do you think it would be suitable for your journal?' One even allows inexperienced authors to send him an article that they are not confident about having properly refereed, in order to get 'preliminary feedback before submitting officially', although other editors would not welcome this.

The matchmaker

One of the editor's key roles (a crucial one for the author) is to match a submission to the referees. Most keep a list or a database of referees and their areas of interests and expertise:

Each referee is asked to identify their areas of expertise and special interest. Papers are matched to the list.

I match by making a best guess from referees' interests; and a balance between someone who is likely to respond and who has not had too many demands made of them recently . . . Occasionally I take advice from the publisher or go to someone in the citations.

Submissions are matched to referees by field, using a database, but I often ring referees in advance of sending them a paper. I try not to use people too often – they are often refereeing elsewhere too. About twice a year, mostly.

The arbiter, where the buck stops

Referees don't always agree; editors may sometimes disagree with and over-rule referees; but the editor has to have the final word:

I've had the classic Yes, No, Maybe, from three different referees. And that happens not infrequently. Sometimes, if I'm not really sure, I'll send it out to a fourth reviewer. But that doesn't always clarify matters!

Disagreements are not always straightforward:

Some disagreements can be 'creative disagreements'. And disagreements are quite nuanced sometimes. And then sometimes referees are not tuned in to editorial policy – they forget it. I sometimes get a third opinion, usually from the executive board.

When two referees disagree, the paper is sent to a third. But ultimately the editor has to make a decision. I have over-ruled referees, especially when one says 'Reject' and the other says 'Accept with minor amendments.'

I am the final arbiter when (rarely) referees disagree fundamentally. I have been known to over-rule referees (but only once or twice – I respect their opinions). I do check that modifications have been made.

The manager

One editor talked of being a 'dogsbody'; another spoke of doing 'humdrum things', of managing everything ('You can't *not* publish'). A job common to all is checking that modifications have been made by an author according to referees' comments.

More than one editor was sceptical about how much power and influence an editor really has: 'My power is more "symbolic" than "actual".' He tries not to over-rule referees. With such a broad range of contributions, he relies heavily on referees and therefore does *not* see himself as a gatekeeper. He has a clear administrative role because he has no formal secretarial support. The publishers do help, but 'with more secretarial support, we could develop the journal more'.

The shaper

Other editors see themselves as shaping or developing a particular field or even 'guarding it'.

> I think it's to help to define the direction of the field . . . An opportunity to lead the way forward, by commissioning articles, special issues, and trying to encourage particular sorts of debates. In practice, though, you're quite constrained in that, because you're really dependent on the types of papers coming in. And you're also constrained by the reviews – in practice I wouldn't want to over-ride the advice of the reviewers too much. In practice you don't have the amount of freedom that people think journal editors do have.

The same editor talked of

> guarding the quality, guarding the identity of a particular field. And with history of education, which has been pretty 'embattled' in institutions of HE, a journal is one of the key sites for the maintenance of the integrity and identity of the field. The journal is prospering and expanding at a time when history of education as a field has been shrinking.

The bearer of news to the author

Most editors see themselves as a kind of mediator between referee and writer, a person who can offer guidance and support rather than harsh rejection:

> I don't just copy opposing viewpoints and send them straight to the author. I've been the victim of that myself – it's very confusing and can be very alienating if you're not used to journals, if the editor simply sends you these opposing viewpoints and says 'sort it out yourself'. I try to go through the reviewers' comments and guide the author to the most important points . . . and I'll add a few of my own to try to point the way forward.

> My policy has always been, if I possibly could, to give people another chance. Even if the reviewers are very critical, I'll send them back and

say 'have another go at it'. People often take six months or even a year to have another go and it could be almost a different paper by the time it comes back. Then I'll send it out to reviewers again and they could easily have to revise it again. Whereas some other journals might say 'There's no chance, we've got too many papers anyway', and send them a reject.

You have to be incredibly considerate for any author, about how you feed back. The only authors I'm short with, blunt and straightforward, are those who ignore referees' comments.

Some editors are less likely to soften the blow:

Some reviews have been dismissive in tone, but we have shared those with authors. This is our policy.

However, the same editor said (elsewhere in the interview) that she 'writes *individual* letters to contributors giving detailed guidance for resubmission; not standard letters'.

The refereeing process: why have a peer-review process?

Some editors looked at me very strangely as I asked this, implying non-verbally that it is a strange thing to ask. One verbalized this view by asking:

What could be the alternative to peer review?

With others, after a few moments of contemplation, interesting answers were forthcoming:

to get adequate evaluation and assessment of scholarly work by people who are established researchers and scholars, and who are able to make informed and well-respected judgements. It's not unlike reviewing and marking students' work and assignments.

One editor talked of the use of referees and peer review from an *editor's perspective*, in terms of a form of self-protection:

I need and use referees because I don't feel sufficiently expert in all fields of education. I want to relieve myself of the responsibility of making the decision all on my own – I'm not the fount of all wisdom. I don't want to be the sole arbiter. I don't want to be exposed as an editor. I've used the peer-review process to protect myself, and the journal, from charges that we favour certain people.

The dangers of *not* using peer review are of course magnified in fields such as medicine. Some editors see its value largely from the author's point of view:

It stops academics from making fools of themselves – it's for their own protection.

If reviewers do their job well, the author should get good advice on their article, even if it's been rejected.

It ensures that a paper published in the journal meets particular criteria. It's a very useful process for *authors* because they get feedback on their papers as they emerge. Papers are almost always the better for having gone through the peer-review process.

When I was doing my Ph.D., some of the best feedback I got – like an additional form of tutorial support – was that feedback from referees on articles. It helps to refine your thinking if you're engaging in some kind of dialogue with fellows in the same field. I see journals as a cheap form of our own continuing professional development. So I have doubts about all this stuff about making our writing 'user friendly' and 'accessible to teachers'. We are polishing up our own work when we go through these processes. Why else do we do it? When I get comments back, I take from them the bits that will help it. All the articles I've done, I've had good feedback on. It acts as a kind of filtering process; it's been deemed by your peers to be good quality, by people who've got some expertise in this area.

Refereeing helps the reader. There is a level of quality assurance for the papers in a refereed journal – so, as a reader, you don't have to read them with the same level of scrutiny as a document on the Web. It's already been through some sort of screening process. It increases 'the level of trust'/faith from the reader. Part of writing articles is learning how to write articles – and the review process helps people to improve the quality of their writing. It's a formative assessment role. Feedback helps subsequent writing, for other articles too. What would we replace it with? It's partly inertia – but it's hard to see an alternative. Conference proceedings are much harder to read and use because they've not been through the refereeing process.

There needs to be a peer-review process. It makes the articles better. Authors admit that their manuscripts have improved. Most agree with the adage that 'good writing is rewriting'. Peer review helps improve an article, establish it and put a value on it.

It's to ensure the quality of the field. Reviewers have experience of what they feel a 'publishable' piece of work is in this field of study, and they would want to make sure that the journal is continuing to maintain those sorts of standards. They would also want to make sure that it's alert to points of style, points of current debate, and those sorts of things.

One editor described the process as serving to 'protect the editor, and protect the author – from their own folly'.

There were some criticisms of practical aspects of the peer-review process, however:

> I am concerned about peer review as a process. Some referees write four lines; others write three pages. Certain referees engage with the process at a much higher level of detail than others. I'm also suspicious, sometimes, of a referee knowing the author, through one means or another. Also, some referees create their own criteria entirely, for judging an article. If I've got any doubt, I send it out to another referee.

> Reviewing is not a hard science. You're relying on people's judgements, even if they all use the same criteria.

Anonymity and masking referees

Most referees (except in two of my cases) do not know who the author of the paper is, but they can often make a good guess:

> It takes the referees about twenty seconds, quite often, to guess the author. Usually, if there are five or six references to a person's work that are favourable . . . or if there's a couple of references to a very obscure Ph.D. thesis, that'll be a giveaway as well.

In one of the cases where referees do see the author's name, the editor saw one disadvantage as creating 'deference':

> Some referees can be very deferential if they know it's a distinguished professor of education writing . . . they're a bit hesitant. And I can be, as an editor.

One journal goes to great lengths to disguise the name of the author from referees, and even the editor herself. The administrator who receives the paper blanks out the author's name before it goes to the editor and thence the referees – in addition, authors who cite themselves (a common practice) are asked to blank out their own name in the references and the text.

What about the other side of the coin? Should authors be allowed to know who is judging their work? The answer was 'no' in most cases, with some caveats:

> Open/visible refereeing might make it even harder to get referees (it's been especially hard to get them in the last few years) and three referees used for every paper. Blind refereeing allows people to be more direct and honest. One idea might be to have two categories of comment, with one category for the editor's eyes only.

> People would badger referees and that would make them harder to get.

In practice, 'Often, experienced authors will guess who the referees are, once they get the comments back.' Finally, from a legal viewpoint, it should be noted that the Data Protection Act prevents publishers from revealing who the referees for specific articles are.

Criteria used by referees and editors: explicit and implicit, 'good' and 'bad'

Some journals do publish, on a web page or on paper, the criteria by which articles submitted are judged (or should be judged) by referees. Some have discussed doing this and have decided against it, having weighed up arguments for and against it. So in a sense, all journals are operating with implicit and explicit criteria. I explored these in interviews and was given some interesting responses.

What counts as a good article?

> Clear and coherent argument backed up by appropriate data (where relevant) well set out.

> Reviewers are guided to comment on lucidity of expression, originality and relevance to journal policy; though I never send them anything that goes completely against the grain of editorial policy, e.g. it's not 'internationalized' or it doesn't discuss a 'big issue'.

> Internal consistency; 'soundness'; is it well written? Does it flow? . . . but all articles are different.

> They should be serious without being solemn. There can be humour, but there can't be lack of substance.

[Explicitly:] Coherence, clarity, interpretation of data, presentation. [Implicitly:] Overall 'feel'.

Reads well, lucid, well organized. Clear evidence of existing knowledge of the topic under investigation; evidence of critical engagement with that and where it will take them; the ability to theorize; to understand the sensitivities of research findings; takes notice of the requirements of the journal.

For a professional journal:

It has to impinge in some way on the subject and pedagogical knowledge of the teachers involved. Now, that's a broad remit! It must address the audience.

A good article makes a significant contribution to the field, is clearly grounded theoretically, has appropriate methodology, explicitly outlined, shows *how* the data have been analysed, is appropriately critical, 'forges new ground', creates new areas for debate, opens up new questions and is clearly written and accessible.

It is _____'s intention that reports of experimental work should be analytical, not merely descriptive; reviews of developing fields should be critical, not merely informative; theoretical overviews should contain some original contribution or novel perspective. Ideally an article would also be well written, clearly structured, novel, well supported and of importance and interest to a majority of our readers. Clearly that's a tall order, and some flexibility may be needed, especially if the article has some redeeming qualities of a different kind.

. . . suitable for an international audience. There have to be broad implications from it. A really good article is trying to do something *different* and new – either in terms of its topic or its methods. Even if the reviewers don't always see it as I would, I'll try to make sure, if I can, that we find a space for those sorts.

A good literature review engages with the methodological issues . . . authors who really operate in a known context, they're not just doing their own little bit in school X, they've taken on the broader picture. It shows how it locates itself within the field, then you can see where it's coming from and what the new insights are.

What we look for is high-quality, well-written, well-rounded, interesting, original, well-organized articles that will appeal to a wide audience. We get some articles which are bad because they lack some, or all, of those qualities. They're not well written, not saying anything new, have a poor literature base and so on. The criteria we apply are derived from the conventional academic virtues.

One editor listed (orally) some of the common terms of praise or buzz words used by referees:

original, exciting contribution, theoretically smart, innovative, challenging, provocative.

What are grounds for rejection? And common complaints?

Where the article doesn't seem to address the majority reader at all, where you just can't see the point of it, you couldn't see how anybody could be enlightened or edified by it at all.

Bad ones: lack any theoretical depth, are not grounded in previous literature, their methodology is inappropriate for the research questions, have short conclusions or discussion, are *just* aimed at classroom practice but not grounded in any theoretical perspective, show little depth of analysis, 'superficial analysis of data'.

(Incidentally, this editor challenged the assumption that teachers don't, or can't, read articles with underpinning theory, and 'the simplistic dichotomy' between 'academic' and 'professional' audiences.)

Insufficient engagement with relevant literature, often from overseas contributions; lacks originality: it's all been said before; does not draw out practical or policy consequences.

Really bad?: the author has never opened the pages of this journal. Someone who has written on a topic and made no reference to a series of articles on the same topic. I can just look at the list of references to get a feel for this.

Confused or incoherent writing, no data or evidence, confusing presentation of data.

No data, poor presentation or interpretation of data, lack of clarity in writing.

. . . if you don't really know what it's about. If it goes all over the place, if it's not sustained, if you can't really see the forms, what's the point? Those are the ones that take two or more goes to hammer them into shape.

Not contextualized, for example the North Americans are writing stuff (in this journal's particular field) that we were writing about ten years ago. They don't read anybody outside North America.

The major problem is that sometimes authors get lost in their own words. Things just don't make sense. Sometimes the conclusions people draw are just not warranted by the discussion they've had beforehand. Sometimes they don't refer to other things that people have done.

Not up-to-date with recent literature on the topic, although it may have some good data; it's not contextualized in its *own* context, e.g. its broader social or historical context.

Very often the data are not analysed sufficiently – referees want a deeper analysis.

Not theorized, too descriptive.

Poorly presented, badly written, inadequately argued, lacking a theoretical framework, uninformed by the literature . . . and so on.

Keeping referees to task: a fine balance

Editors recognize that there is a delicate balance between keeping things moving for authors and yet not putting too much pressure on their referees.

It is becoming increasingly common for referees to refuse and difficult to get new referees.

But some editors take a hard line:

If a reviewer should prove to be unreliable on three occasions, then we'd just say 'thanks very much for your services'. As a new journal we want a reputation for dealing with people professionally.

Some referees don't do their job. In the long term, I eliminate those people. Often, it's the big names.

Referees have to be reliable in terms of the period of turnaround. Papers have to be turned round within three weeks of receipt. Failure to meet those deadlines three times means instant dismissal from the board. We won't carry people.

Expectations were equally clear in another case:

People on the editorial board are expected to review about five articles per annum and attend an annual meeting. If they don't do their job, 'we invite them to withdraw'.

Reviewers are expected to return an article within three weeks. Often they don't and are sent a reminder. If they don't meet deadlines, they are marked people.

However, editors do realize that they are hugely dependent on their referees:

I tell them four weeks and some referees are really good. You always get to know who's going to do it on time. Others certainly take their time. You're always dependent on your reviewers. Usually I send them a polite e-mail, and usually that's enough. You don't really have any sanctions over them, it's all their good will, and they don't get any Brownie points for it . . . you're trying to get them to do you a favour. You soon learn which referees will do things most quickly. And that's *another issue*, because once you do find out who is reliable, you tend to rely on them more, and potentially that's a limiting factor in the development of the field. You have to stop yourself relying on a few old cronies all the time!

Time lags in getting published

Of course, the other factor that can slow publication down is the rate at which an author responds to comments and suggestions:

Some authors can take up to two years to revise a paper. We don't put a time limit on authors. I always say 'take your time, give it your best shot'.

The other key variable in determining the time lapse from submission to publication is the amount of material (copy) waiting in the system:

The delay could easily be eighteen months. We're at least a year ahead of ourselves. A year is a healthy one – much more than that and it starts to get out of date. Much less, and you get really worried about shortage of copy. It's a fine balance. I was able to make a case for expanding the journal to six issues only because we had so much good copy coming in.

This editor had been asked, prior to the last Research Assessment Exercise, if they could in effect 'jump the queue', using questions such as 'Can it be published before such and such a date?' The editor would not assent: 'I won't shuffle the pack.'

In short, there is a fine line, which editors must follow, between having so much copy in the pipeline that authors are kept waiting for many months or even two years, and having so little in reserve that they are worrying about filling the next issue. Keeping on the right side of this line can be very difficult for the editor, especially when there are 'blips in the amount of copy', as one put it. From an author's point of view, it can be highly frustrating if a piece of work is finally accepted (perhaps after the author has waited patiently for refereeing and then has had to make amendments) and then a delay of eighteen months to two years follows before it appears in print. However, an author might well be suspicious of a journal, its attraction for authors and its status if an article appears in print barely a month after final acceptance.

Going electronic

None of the editors in my sample had any plans to go completely electronic, i.e. to abandon the print-on-paper version. Most were uncertain of how journals would evolve in the future.

> The publishers are as unsure as we are about what the future holds.

> I don't know what I think about this. I'm more comfortable with the traditional *embodiment* of a journal. The holding of the book is still, culturally, what people prefer to do. They're an embodiment; I prefer that physical, non-virtual embodiment.

> In all cases, institutions can subscribe to on-line versions of the journal, but there are no plans to abandon the print version, in part because of the RAE requirements here and overseas, and in part because some of our readers do not have easy on-line access to anything.

One editor could see clearly the advantages of an e-version:

> The e-version of the journal includes things that cannot be put into print, e.g. video, audio. But we are *not* planning to abandon print, largely because of global accessibility.

Some journals are beginning to handle everything from the submission stage through to final copy electronically, but others were reluctant to abandon the traditional submission of 'three hard copies sent by post to the editor'. One reason given is that the path of the article through the system is then easier to keep an eye on:

> I like being sent paper copy as I would print submissions out to read them anyway. There are still some technical issues which would reduce flexibility (e.g. requiring web forms for referees' comments). The publishers

do not want to move to electronic handling yet. Some referees would want this; some vehemently do not.

In contrast, one editor welcomes electronic handling:

> Papers are sent to reviewers electronically. Most reviewers are happy with that, but one reviewer has asked for paper copies. I don't see any problems with electronic submissions at all. It also makes it much easier to anonymize papers before refereeing. [The Secretary does this, so that even the editor does not know the author's identity.]

Another had moved almost entirely to electronic handling:

> We prefer electronic submissions. Hard copy is only used in extremes if the author has no e-mail. We handle everything up to and including return of proofs electronically.

How do editors see themselves and their position?

Views vary on this. Some editors play down their position, describing their power as more 'symbolic' than 'actual' and emphasizing their dependence on referees.

> I think it's to help to define the direction of the field . . . an opportunity to lead the way forward, by commissioning articles, special issues, and trying to encourage particular sorts of debates. In practice, though, you're quite constrained in that, because you're really dependent on the types of papers coming in. And you're also constrained by the reviews – in practice I wouldn't want to over-ride the advice of the reviewers too much. In practice you don't have the amount of freedom that people think journal editors do have.

Another editor used the term 'hassled dogsbody'. In contrast, one interviewee talked of being an editor as 'a great professional position to be in'. Another described her job as 'very rewarding, very enjoyable'. Most seem to have a mixture of feelings, the positive outweighing the negative, for example:

> I enjoy it up to a point – but it's a job that I do in addition to all the other things I do. I have to do it in whatever spare time I've got, so it is a bit of a chore sometimes. I enjoy the inevitable networking that results from it. You get to know a lot of people, referees and authors. I wish I had more time to enjoy it. To enable somebody who has written something, to have it published and disseminated widely is a great privilege. It's a privilege to be a facilitator or a conduit for someone's work.

Some editors were totally positive:

> I get to read stuff two years before anyone else sees it. I enjoy working with new authors too.

> I love the job. In association with others, you can contribute to the development of a field and give opportunities to new scholars.

The traditional model of 'gatekeeper' was not favoured as the main metaphor for their role:

> I enjoy the job, which I would describe as an enhancer.

> Gatekeeper – I don't think so. That's more about rejection than acceptance. The refereeing process does make things better. Referees aren't rejecting because they don't want to see things in print – they're rejecting because they can see it, imagine it written better, they want to see it improved.

> I do open doors for people. I heard someone present a paper at a conference and I asked her to submit it to the journal. I only *close* the gate when somebody is trying to trespass, who is trying to persuade me, because of their eminence usually, that what they've sent to me is by definition good. The fact that it doesn't articulate remotely with our editorial policy, the fact that it's written on the proverbial back of an envelope, they see as neither here nor there! I'm quite sharp about it: I don't want to be seen as a soft touch. I want to maintain the highest standards.

> I see myself as a facilitator, a shaper, forging a new, emerging field and challenging some of the boundaries in ____ [name of the field].

> I am creating opportunities for people to make their work public.

> I'd like to think of myself as a good mentor, a mediator. But a good mentor is also going to serve as a gatekeeper. Decisions have to be made; we only accept about one out of every three articles.

> One is a gatekeeper, but I'm a facilitator, I think, for sending out people's work to a wider audience. In a way, I'm closing the gate to some people. But I'd much rather encourage the view that I'm promoting good work and that's what it's about. I don't know – an 'enhancer'. One isn't only a gate, one's a bridge, often between communities.

I don't like to see us as gatekeeping, except in the most democratic way we possibly can. I see journals as part of our academic development.

The last word . . .

In many ways the voices of the editors speak for themselves and need no support or attempt to summarize from me. But I am the author so I will have a brief last word.

Editors do follow different practices and use slightly different criteria, but there is a lot of common ground. The one thing they all have in common, of course, is the ability to articulate clearly and with conviction the benefits of a peer-review system – these benefits extend not only to the development of a research community and a field of study or scholarship but also to authors themselves, in making their papers better. They are able to recognize the drawbacks and difficulties in peer review, but all see it as (at the very least) the 'best system we have got'. Again, editors do see their roles in slightly different ways: most do act as an initial filter, but all rely on the expertise and valued judgement of their referees. Some see themselves as gatekeepers, but my impression in meeting them face to face was that they see nothing sinister about this role. All editors see themselves equally as enhancers, improvers, disseminators, shapers of a field, mentors and mediators.

Chapter 5

Book publishing

Producing a book is often viewed as a more daunting task than writing and publishing a journal article. Without doubt, it requires considerably more work – but in many ways the refereeing process is less arduous, especially once a writer has something of a track record. This chapter explores the issues involved in book publishing and offers practical guidance from different sources, including book publishers themselves. The first part of the chapter, like the first part of Chapter 4, is written from the author's perspective. The second part of the chapter looks inside the reviewing and editing processes that take place inside the publishing house. The last section includes views collected from some of the major UK book publishers on the current influences driving this area, with speculations on the future.

FROM THE AUTHOR'S PERSPECTIVE

Books and where they come from

In many circles book writing has been seen as the pinnacle of academic achievement. Powell's (1985) study of book publishing is prefaced by this eulogy:

> For the community of American scholars, books are very important commodities. They are written, read, debated and reviewed. Reputations are tied to the success or failure of one's latest book. Promotion, tenure and even one's first job are tied to the quality of one's writing. Publishing is the primary measure of academic achievement. A few scholars and unattached individuals command so significant an audience that their writings are also a source of considerable income. So, for the academic community, books serve a highly utilitarian purpose, and it is scholarly publishing houses that are the gatekeepers to this important medium of communication.

I like this passage partly because of its 'over the top' praise, verging on hyperbole, for the importance of the book. This reverence for the book is now far more contested and contestable – some would argue that the print-on-paper book has had its heyday, and we look at this in Chapter 7. Some might also argue that academic status is now conferred less by a commercially published book (especially a textbook) than by articles published in 'eminent, high-status journals'. Again, we leave this debate for now, returning to it at the end of this chapter. I also like Powell's passage for its use, once again, of the gate-keeper metaphor. We look into the role of 'gatekeepers' in later sections, but first a short discussion of where books might come from.

A book from a thesis

For many authors (including me), their first academic book is a by-product of their Master's or doctoral thesis. Woods (1999: 113) argues that all theses at Master's level and above 'should contain at least one potential article'. I would agree with this, provided that the thesis does contribute to public knowledge and not solely the student's own personal and professional development. Equally, many theses have the potential to be transformed into a book. The article or book is unlikely to have the extensive data presentation, tables of results, comprehensive literature review, methodology discussion, appendices and plethora of references that would be expected in a doctoral thesis – but its central themes, its original contribution to knowledge (expected of theses by most examination boards) and its innovative ideas and discussion are all likely to interest a book publisher.

So the task of converting a thesis into a book is not a small one. It involves radical changes to the content, including much chopping down. A new title will be needed, agreeable to the publisher. The audience and therefore the style of writing will be different. In short, it requires severe editing, extensive rewriting and certainly a large element of 'repackaging'. Eggleston and Klein (1997: 33) call this process 'recasting', and they give valuable practical guide-lines on how to do it (pp. 33–36). Deats (1997) has also written useful guidance on converting a dissertation to a book, advocating that authors need to assume 'an entirely new perspective towards the subject matter and the reader, perhaps allowing for a waiting period before undertaking this daunting task' (p. 137). She also refers to Holmes' advice from the 1970s, which still holds good. Holmes' three articles (1974 and 1975) gave tips on 'what to get rid of', e.g.: excessive surveys of the literature and 'gratuitous quoting'; wordy, circuitous openings and recapitulations of what has been covered so far; and 'apologetic disclaimers' telling the examiners what has *not been* covered. Holmes' third article on this (1975) tells the writer 'what to do with what is left', stressing 'clarity, concreteness, pace and a climactic conclusion'.

A book from scratch

Sometimes a book (or an article) may appear to 'start from scratch', but in reality there is usually a source, a seed, a stimulus, a spark or a catalyst that brings the idea for a book and the consequent book to life. (This, and all the points in this paragraph, apply equally to a journal article, of course.) For example, it may be a paper that one has listened to, an article one has read, a conference attended, a paper given or heard at conference, a seminar attended or presented, another book, or a teaching session one has given. Comments and feedback from an audience at a conference, a seminar or a teaching session can often be the vital spark. The thought may then occur: that would make an excellent theme for an article or a book (either authored or edited). Once the initial idea takes hold, it may then grow into material for a book that an author collects until there is enough substance to form a book proposal for a publisher. My own way of working is gradually to build up material by a process of accretion (filed in cardboard boxes or arch files) that forms the foundation of the book. The boxes may contain photocopied readings, books, journals, notes and jottings or the embryos of some of the chapters. On the word processor I create a new directory for it (using a really imaginative file name like 'New Book') and use it to stash away any useful electronic material towards the book, including my own bits of writing, provisional contents and plan, and useful websites or other electronic references. The combination of accreting material in cardboard boxes and electronic material on the hard disc can be enough to convince me that there may be enough of a source to lead to a book. The next stage is then to write to a publisher and try to convince them (discussed later in this chapter).

Authors, especially if they have a good track record, may sometimes be approached by a publisher (usually the commissioning editor) to see if they would like to write a book on a certain topic. This may occur at a conference (if, say, a paper you have presented has impressed the audience), or it may occur at a meeting. Many commissioning editors 'do the rounds' of university and college departments as part of their networking role (see Powell's study later). This is as important for them as it is for you; so don't hesitate to arrange a meeting on one of these visits. They may ask you to suggest where you think there may be a gap in their 'list' and perhaps invite you to submit a proposal for a book that might fill it. The importance of your own personal contacts and networking, at meetings and at conferences, should not be underestimated.

Other ways of doing it

A third way is to write a series of articles and then to bring them together to form a book. This is easier if all the articles have a similar theme that can be used as a unifier. Of course, if an author uses substantial amounts of previously published work, even in a rephrased form, in a later publication, then permission is needed. This is usually not a problem. Others have written chapters in different books and then decided to pull them all together and produce a book.

There is some cynicism about the issue of recycling one's own work, especially when it can be viewed as a ploy for apparently increasing an academic's output for a forthcoming Research Assessment Exercise. The term 'self-plagiarism' has even been used. This cynicism is understandable. I have seen articles in different journals that are almost identical except for the title and perhaps slight differences in emphasis. I have had first-hand experience of a similar ploy with book editing. I once edited a book for a major publisher that included one very good chapter from a colleague in another university. As fate would have it, I was asked by a journal to review an edited book on the same theme two years later. One of the chapters in the book was identical (word for word) to the chapter in my edited book, apart from the title. The author had reused the chapter without acknowledging that it had been published before.

My own view is that recycling and reworking previous writing so that it is published in a new form such as a book can be an acceptable practice, provided that authors are honest about it, and all necessary permissions are obtained. A book containing ideas and writing from (say) previously published articles can be a useful new synthesis or re-presentation of someone's work, often in a new form, sometimes far more accessible and readable than a scattering of articles and thoughts in different publications, sometimes hard to obtain. The simple fact that all the work is presented to a high, consistent standard under one cover can provide added value.

Choosing a publisher

Despite all the takeovers and reshuffling that seem to be endemic to the industry, there is still a good range of publishers for an author to turn to. Current information on all these publishers can be obtained from their websites or their printed catalogues.

Many of the same questions are raised in deciding which publisher to target as in deciding which journal to aim for. Should I go for the most prestigious? Or would I have more chance of publication by aiming for a smaller, lesser-known organization? Is there a hierarchy or pecking order amongst publishers? If so, on which criteria is this order based? If I want to maximize the readership of my work, should I aim for the publisher with the best marketing, sales and promotion 'machine' – and will this publisher be the same as the top ranked in the 'quality pecking order'? Do different fields within the same broad area or discipline, e.g. literacy, inclusive education, science or ICT within education, have different hierarchies? Are certain publishers best, and more likely to consider a proposal seriously, in certain fields? Or is it best to go for the best 'general publisher' in the discipline, regardless of the field within it?

Consider too your own views of the existing titles, the reputation and the image of the publisher. Do you find their books valuable, well written, scholarly, well produced and well presented? Have they marketed their list well to you personally (as a student, a lecturer or whatever)? Are they visible at the conferences that you attend or even in your own department? Which authors have written, and continue to write, for them? These are all questions that need to be posed. I don't have clear or final answers to them, and no clear answers are forthcoming in the literature, largely because specific answers to each question will depend on the specifics of each case – in targeting it is a matter of choosing the right horse for the right course.

Haynes (2001), himself a commissioning editor for a major publisher, gives excellent practical advice on selecting a publisher for your idea or proposal: 'the first job is to discover which publishers are active in the field in which you wish to publish'. This is similar to the situation in selecting a target journal. There are many printed and on-line reference sources that can help potential authors to do this (Haynes suggests: www.library.vanderbilt.edu/law/acqs/ pubr.html). Also, consult your colleagues and peers – which publishers have they worked with and why? What have been their experiences? Lecturers will also find it useful to consult or canvass students' opinions on different publishers. Investigate which publishers are most active in the types of market that form your intended readership. Examine some of their recent books. Haynes suggests that the ideal target is 'a publisher that has several books that are comparable to yours, but nothing quite the same'. Speaking from his experience as a commissioning editor, Haynes advises that even where the publisher's list of existing books includes one almost identical to your own proposal, the firm may still be worth pursuing. For example, the publisher may not be totally happy with the existing book, or it may be going out of date, or (on closer scrutiny) the two books could be slightly different and could complement, rather than compete with, each other.

In an interesting ethnographic study of two book publishers, Powell (1985) reports on the importance of informal networks and contacts in book publishing. Powell talks of one of the key roles of the acquisitions/commissioning editor being to create and maintain these networks, grapevines and contacts. Publishers need authors as much as we need them. The editor needs to: keep up with developing areas in the discipline; know the 'leading scholars'; meet the 'new people' in a field and know the new, growth areas; establish good relationships with authors; stay informed about new lines of research; find new, 'fresh' authors; and finally, have a strong network of advisers to draw upon in reviewing and assessing new book proposals. The editor can only achieve this by 'getting out and talking to people' (Powell, 1985: 81). Editors want to meet you as much as you want to meet them – authors should make use of this.

Series or parallel submissions: books compared with journals

The one apparent advantage that would-be authors have in the ethics of the book world over those submitting to a journal is something that I call parallel processing. In other words, writers can submit a book proposal to as many publishers as they like at once. These publishers can then be considering the proposal in parallel, rather than one after the other (in series) as journal editors expect to do. It is deemed unethical to submit an article to more than one journal at a time – many journals now require a written statement in a covering letter to the effect that the paper is not being considered elsewhere.

I do know people who have submitted the same article to more than one journal at once, and still do. Their argument is that they cannot afford to wait for the process to go through one journal after another, in a series. They seem to be prepared to risk the annoyance of journal editors and the possibility of receiving egg on their faces. I must admit that I once did a similar thing myself when I gave up on one journal after waiting about six months for a reply, and sent the same article to another journal. As fate would have it, both accepted it (the second after the long delay, the first very quickly). I was left to write a very obsequious letter of apology to the first, who will doubtless be very reluctant to consider anything in the future with my name on it. I have never done this since. Most editors consider simultaneous submissions to more than one journal as not only unethical but extremely annoying and time wasting.

Book publishers do not take quite the same stance. Many now anticipate (or suspect) that a book proposal is being sent to several targets at the same time. However, they do like to be told if this is the case. This may appear to be a big advantage for an author in that parallel processing can occur, as opposed to the lengthy process of perhaps being rejected by one journal (after several months) and then having to revise for another target and wait again for the refereeing process to take its course.

However, it is important to weigh up the pros and cons of submitting book proposals to more than one publisher at a time. Clearly, time is the apparent advantage of parallel processing. But there are several persuasive reasons for not approaching publishers simultaneously. Firstly, it may make the commissioning editor reluctant to invest time and reviewer money in judging the proposal. Secondly, it might cause ill feeling and mistrust. But most importantly, submitting a proposal to one at a time gives the author an ideal opportunity to receive valuable, free feedback on the proposal. Rejection often comes with reviewers' comments, evaluations and suggestions – the author can take these on board in making the second version better. My own verdict is that it is best to approach only one publisher at a time. The publishers of this book tell me that authors who ignore this advice take the risk of irritating a publisher by wasting their time and money, blotting their own copybook and tarnishing their reputation.

Writing and submitting a proposal

My view is that you should never write a book before seeking and finding a publisher, having your proposal scrutinized and advised upon, and then receiving a contract safely in your hand. As Woods (1999) points out, writing a book is hard and time-consuming work; also, going through the proposal and contract stage forces you to think long and hard about the style, content, market and readership of the book.

It is sometimes best to send in an initial inquiry to a publisher or publishers to see if they might be interested in your idea or proposal. This quickly tells you which publishers would definitely not be interested in seeing a full proposal. Haynes (2001: 35) discusses this in his usual valuable and honest discussion of this. His own opinion as a commissioning editor is that inquiry letters are of little value. They do not give enough detail to allow an editor to make any decision, so 'why not just send the proposal in the first place?'

Usually, a proposal will consist of a synopsis of the book and one or two sample chapters. This section discusses in detail exactly what such a proposal might contain. First it is worth noting Powell's (1985: 87) observation that if the entire typescript of a book is sent in it indicates one of two possibilities: either the author is a young, inexperienced person (e.g. has just finished a Ph.D.), or the author is an experienced, esteemed academic who 'has written the whole thing, confident that someone will publish it'.

So what would a typical proposal look like? There is a fair measure of agreement amongst different publishers on this. Haynes (2001) suggests that a publisher needs to know at least seven things. I have adapted his list as follows:

- The provisional title of the book
- Its proposed contents: what will the book be about?
- The market: who is going to buy it?
- The competition: how will it compare with, compete with or complement existing books?
- Who is the author?
- The timescale: when will the script be ready?
- Production requirements: how long will it be (the extent); how many tables, illustrations, etc., will it contain?

These aspects of the proposal are all-important and so are now discussed more fully. Firstly, the title is worth careful thought, even though it is provisional and will probably change. A title for a book is perhaps more important than for a journal article. It should be attractive and yet descriptive. Cryptic titles are not helpful, nor are titles that are trying to sound too clever or erudite. The use of main title followed by a colon and a sub-title has become a bit hackneyed, but it often works for the provisional title for a proposal. Secondly, content can be outlined by giving a provisional contents list with headings and sub-headings. It is probably not necessary to go down to the level of sub-sub- or sub-sub-sub-headings even if you know them! A few thoughts can then be given on each chapter and related back to a synopsis. Do not include *too much* detail about the contents, neglecting other aspects of the proposal. Authors need to think carefully and carry out some research into the market for a book. They need to be clear and concrete, avoiding blanket terms such as 'Master's students' or 'undergraduates'. Be specific and beware of claiming too broad a market – this will not be plausible. If possible, quantify the market by looking up recent data on numbers of students, researchers or lecturers in the proposed areas. For a course text, how many students were studying this in the last cohort and in how many institutions? Will the book be valuable in the UK or will it only appeal in England? What is the potential in the USA and other English-speaking countries such as Australia? Does it have potential in the East, e.g. Singapore, Hong Kong, China? Could it ever break into the European market?

Assessing competition

Authors need to be critical here, but not dismissive or unfair. If you scathingly criticize all competition in the area, then you may appear pompous, implausible and, worse still, *naïve*. Your evaluation of the 'opposition' should be balanced, thorough and honest, and above all precise. What is good about some of the books in print, but what could be better? Exactly why is your book an improvement on existing titles? Haynes talks of putting a USP in your proposal: what is your Unique Selling Point?

You as the author

What can you say about yourself that does not sound like false modesty or humility, yet does not feel pompous and conceited? Track record, previous publications, research and/or teaching experience should all be relevant. Include associations and networks that you belong to that might help in both writing and eventual marketing of the book. A full CV may well be too long, so pick out the achievements pertinent to this proposal. As for timescale, be realistic, not optimistic. Don't underestimate the time it takes to put a book together. Allow time for the tedious bits such as checking references, checking your typing, and redrafting or reformatting. Allow time for unexpected events at work or at home. Start the time plan from the expected date of receiving a contract, rather than the date of sending in the proposal. Contracts take time to arrive, even after an editor has said 'yes'.

Sample chapters

This is always a fuzzy one – some editors will insist on at least two sample chapters, especially if you have not written for them before. Once you have a track record, the demand for sample writing may ease. (I have been given book contracts without having included any sample chapters with the proposal.) Editors often require them for two main reasons: to see if you can write well, especially if you are a new author; and to show more fully what the book is about, to see if it does indeed match the proposed market readership. If you are asked for two chapters, provide the introductory one and one other chapter. Box 5.1 shows my own distillation from the guidelines issued to prospective authors by major publishers.

Box 5.1 gives a fairly comprehensive summary of the key elements needed for a good book proposal. One final point: send your proposal to a named person if you possibly can, not just 'The Editor', and include a short covering letter. Don't sound too pushy or pompous, but don't grovel.

Box 5.1 Preparing a book proposal: a summary of guidelines given by publishers

---

1 *Proposed title*
Suggest a provisional title that reflects the content, the approach and the aims of the proposed text in relation to the intended reader.

2 *Synopsis (500–1,000 words in length)*
Include brief statements on:

- The topic: the subject of the book, courses it is intended for and the level
- The aims of the book: what does it propose to do? Why is there a need for this book? How will the book achieve its aims?
- Scope and coverage: what is included/excluded and why?
- Price: what would you consider to be a competitive price for the text?
- A short paragraph which sums up the proposed book without using jargon (a 'soundbite', as some publishers call it).

3 *Length, illustrations and permissions*
Give the anticipated word length of the proposed book. Will it include any figures, graphs, illustrations, etc.? Will any of these come from other sources and therefore need permission?

4 *Contents list*
Give an annotated contents list, showing the chapter/book structure and organization clearly, and a summary (approximately 100–150 words per chapter) of the main issues to be covered in each chapter.

5 *Interesting features*
Provide a list of any interesting features that will be included in the text (e.g. boxed summaries, end-of-chapter summaries, case studies, tables, graphs or illustrations, a glossary, annotated bibliography or ideas for further reading).

continued on next page

Box 5.1 continued from previous page

6 *The market/intended readership*

– What are the primary and the secondary markets for the book?
– Does the book have an international market?
– What gap or niche does your book seek to fill?
– On what courses would the book be used?
– How quickly is the book likely to date?
– What is the scope of the market in terms of a rough indication of student numbers? UK only? USA? Europe? Global?
– How could the publishers inform the potential market about the book?

7 *Competing texts/existing books in the area*

– List and describe books currently on the market, giving as many details as possible: author name; title; publisher; publication date; extent; price; strengths and weaknesses.
– Show how your title will differ from the competing texts. What do you consider to be the advantages/disadvantages of your text over these? What makes it *different*?

8 *Timetable/writing plan*
Give a realistic prediction of the expected writing schedule and provisional delivery date for the entire typescript.

9 *Sample material*
If possible, supply one or two draft chapters (often an introductory chapter and one other) to provide referees with a sense of the proposed text and an indication of writing style and level.

10 *The author's/authors' mini-CV or CVs*
Include the following details for all of the authors involved in the proposed book: full name(s); contact details (address, telephone and fax numbers, e-mail); qualifications; present appointments; career to date; previous publications.

11 *Potential referees*
If possible, give the names and contact details of people in the field who might act as referees.

What happens to the proposal?

Editors tend to act as a preliminary filter (as they do with journals). Their initial questions are likely to be: Who will read this and buy it? Is it well written? How much work (for the publisher) is required in producing and publishing it? Does it make 'a substantial intellectual contribution' (Powell, 1985)? They will not send out 'junk' (as Powell, 1985: 103 put it), but they will (unlike journal editors) occasionally make encouraging noises, e.g. if the proposal has come from a well-known author with a track record. Then the proposal will go out to reviewers, usually two or three. The author may have suggested these; editors may use people they know, who are reliable and efficient, and whose judgement they can trust; they may use reviewers who have been cited in the proposal; or commonly they will use other authors who have 'been published by the house' (Powell, 1985). Reviewers are usually paid a small fee (unlike journal referees) or offered free books from the publisher's list.

The way publishers and commissioning editors make decisions is explored fully in the second part of this chapter.

Practical issues from conception to publication

If a proposal is successful, an author will be offered a contract, which then needs scrutinizing. Check the important points on the contract such as length, submission date, translation rights, number of free copies given, royalties and advances. My own view is that it is not worth paying an agent to advise you, or haggling yourself for a long period, in the hope of gaining a more lucrative contract. This is probably because I measure my own royalties on academic books in units of take-away meals per annum. Most books of this kind (with some notable exceptions) tend not to be bestsellers. Also, most contracts are fairly standard.

Some publishers pay an advance on signature of the contract, then more when you submit the script by post and e-mail. These payments count against your royalties, and my experience is that publishers are quite generous here with academic books. I still receive a royalty statement every year on a book I wrote several years ago with a negative sign against my earnings. In other words, the royalties have not yet overtaken the advance and probably never will – but publishers seem very tolerant about this.

The problem that arises after receiving a contract and signing it is that you are then obliged to write the book. This sometimes comes as a shock after the initial pleasant feeling. In Chapter 6, I talk about the practical aspects of writing, and this should be read with the earlier discussion in Chapter 3. Writers do actually get help from publishers in this process, and it makes sense to seek it and use it. Good publishers provide a comprehensive set of guidelines or instructions for authors (totalling sixty-three pages for this book, from RoutledgeFalmer). These give information on everything from presentation to useful software, legal advice and permission, proofreading and preparing an index – all of which may be the author's responsibility.

Once the text has been submitted to and accepted by the publisher, the valuable ally for the author is the copy-editor, who does you the huge favour of checking every word you have written. He or she will raise a number of queries about your typescript. The list can be quite daunting, ranging from sentences that don't make sense, to headings and sub-headings that are not consistent, to numerous missing references. In my case, the queries about references run to pages – often listing people I have included in the references but not used in the text, or more commonly vice versa. Copy-editors' queries can be a pain when you receive them, but remember (as I said above) to treat them as a favour. If you are writing your thesis you get no such help and double-checking, unless you pay for it.

There are other practical things that authors will commonly need to do. Permissions are usually the responsibility of the author. Obtaining them can be time consuming and costly. If you want to use a newspaper extract or a longish piece (anything more than 400 words) from another work, even your own pre-published work, then you will need to write for permission from the original publisher. Newspapers usually charge a fee, as much as £200 in my experience. Permissions will also be needed for any illustrations, tables or Internet material that you use in your work, even if adapted.

Proofreading and indexing are also the responsibility of the author, although a professional indexer can do the latter if the author wants this and is prepared to pay for it.

Coping with rejection

Not every book proposal that you submit will be successful. I have had my share of success, but one proposal (for an edited book) that I sent in to four publishers in 2001 received four very polite letters of rejection, all from editors who know me well. The reasons given included:

- We have published or have under contract a significant number of books on or about ____, and so we have probably published enough books in this area.
- The market for this book is likely to be somewhat limited.
- As an edited collection, even with some eminent contributors, the proposal is unlikely to sell in large enough quantities to justify publication.
- Not at all sure of the market for this.
- A more general concern over edited books which feature chapters from different subject areas.
- Not for us, for two simple reasons: (1) We've already done two books on ____. (2) I am reluctant to publish edited books.

So, you may need to learn to cope with rejection. Take constructive action (McCallum, 1997). Analyse the proposal and any comments you've received; use them to improve the next version. Don't waste time in writing obstreperous letters back to the editor expressing your amazement that they did not accept you. Persevere. Enid Blyton collected 500 rejections according to McCallum (1997: 62), and look what happened to her much-debated output. This personal confession from Underwood back in 1957 is still helpful to read if you are coping with rejection:

> The rejection of my own manuscripts has a sordid aftermath: (a) one day of depression; (b) one day of utter contempt for the editor and his accomplices; (c) one day of decrying the conspiracy against letting Truth be published; (d) one day of fretful ideas about changing my profession; (e) one day of re-evaluating the manuscript in view of the editor's comments followed by the conclusion that I was lucky it wasn't accepted!
>
> (Underwood, 1957: 87)

Editing books

Producing an edited book is a very different activity from writing a sole or co-authored book, especially when the latter is written from scratch. For example, good writers do not always make the best editors of other people's work (or their own in some cases). I have edited four books with major publishers. My own experience has been an enjoyable one, if a little frustrating at times. I describe these experiences and frustrations under six headings below.

Gaining the interest of a publisher

The first stage, of course, is to interest a publisher. This can only be done, in my experience, by submitting a proposal in the usual way (as discussed above). It has to be a strong proposal – why should it be an edited collection rather than an authored or co-authored book? My recent experience, based on discussions with commissioning editors and one of my own proposals rejected by five different publishers, is that edited books are currently less attractive to publishers than they were perhaps five or ten years ago. A practical complication is that the track record (mini-CVs) of all the authors can help to sell the proposal. Collecting and collating these takes time. Creating the proposal also has to be done concurrently with the business of attracting and handling authors.

Enticing authors

This has generally been a good experience for me, but there are certain hurdles to beware of. Firstly, getting them involved: I have usually done this by phone and e-mail. A combination of flattery and praise for their previous work, mixed with a good explanation of why you particularly want *them* and not some other author, seems to work. The offer of a fee from the publisher does not. Usually the fee is a measly one (typically £40 or £50 per chapter, though I have heard of more). It usually comes out of the editor's royalty, so beware of offering too much unless you want to receive negative royalty statements for some time to come. My experience is that the fee can annoy people as much as entice them.

Handling authors

The next stage is to tell the authors (again by phone and e-mail) pretty much what you want, i.e. the theme, the length, the readership they will be writing for. This stage includes telling them who else will be contributing so that writers can complement each other and cross-refer, as opposed to repeating, or competing with, each other. This is a delicate negotiating stage because authors don't always want to write about what you want them to write about! They often have a pet project or a new idea (or sometimes an old one) that they really want to get into print, and they may see your edited book as the perfect opportunity. High levels of tact and diplomacy are required by an editor to ensure that they get the chapter they want – and the one originally promised to the publisher.

   The editor then needs to receive a synopsis from each author (I suggest about 300 words), similar to the abstract for a thesis in outlining the key themes. These again may need to be negotiated and discussed with each author. The editor's job is then to circulate these to all the authors (assuming that they all come in on time, which can take considerable persuasion and cajoling). This is where e-mail is valuable, not only in speeding up the process but also in allowing discussion and interaction between the authors themselves. Sometime around this phase the author also has to negotiate a contract with the publisher and ask them to sort out individual contracts for each author.

Setting and meeting deadlines

After a reasonable deadline has been set for contributions (I think that a maximum of six months from authors seeing each other's synopsis to submission of the first draft is a rule of thumb), the next stage is to wait for them to arrive (preferably electronically and as hard copy, in my view). This can be a strange six-month period for an editor. Some will submit almost within a fortnight. This at once makes the editor slightly suspicious: is this recycled work which had been waiting for another outlet? Is the author really not that busy? More positively, some authors I have worked with are extremely efficient, and once they are commissioned to write a chapter they get straight on with it. Many of the ideas or data for it may have been ready and waiting. Other authors will either not meet the deadline or ask for an extension. My view is that an editor should not extend deadlines unless the author has a very persuasive case. Offering an extension to one author will be about as popular with the others (who have submitted on time) as offering extensions to students is to classmates who have struggled to submit their coursework on time. Allowing one author the luxury of a few more weeks or even more months (as I know some editors have done) is quite simply unfair on those who are punctual. Everyone's work is delayed, and ill feeling may be created. Using this argument, I once refused to allow a very illustrious author an extension, and the author was quite surprised. In the event, he submitted on time. In another case, an author told me that he could not submit his chapter until two months after the deadline, so I went ahead without it.

Pulling it together

This can be a difficult task for an editor, especially if the original proposal did not have unifying themes that could be used to structure the book and make it both coherent and cogent. As a result, some edited books are little more than a collection of disparate chapters: authors have not referred to each other's work, there are no recurrent themes and the whole thing is a disconnected series. In my view, it is the editor's job to try to keep things together during the writing process by circulating synopses and draft chapters amongst the authors (ideally by e-mail). This may not succeed totally, so (after the event, in a sense) the editor needs to do some extra work – a combination of editing and writing – to produce something resembling a coherent whole. This may necessitate a carefully written preface or an introductory chapter (a kind of prologue); or it may require link sections between chapters or between parts/ sections of the book that are grouped into themes. An edited book may also be improved by a section or even a chapter at the end, trying to pull things together and saying 'Where are we, and so what?' (a kind of epilogue). Either way, the editor has to do some work to avoid the edited book that is just a range of chapters on a very broad theme, brought together under one cover.

Coping with doubts

All writers are beset by doubt; editors suffer from it too. Will the book sell? Why did I go for these authors and not others? Is the book complete, i.e. has it covered all aspects of the theme or issue it purports to cover? Will anyone read it? Will it be of value in a Research Assessment Exercise? I am not quite sure exactly what counts as a good edited book, though I think I know one when I see one.

Smedley (1993: 28) provides a useful discussion of the qualities that editors should aim for in a collection of chapters. To finish this section I offer a summary, based on her work, of some of the key features of a good edited collection (see Box 5.2).

Box 5.2 Key features of a good edited book

1 An edited book should be on a theme or topic where no one author possesses enough knowledge to summarize or synthesize all of the work in that area. Each contributor should provide a piece of 'the puzzle' that no one individual author could provide.
2 It should be as carefully planned and designed by the editor as would an authored book, with chapters flowing logically from one to the other, and linked together. Cross-reference should be made between chapters.
3 The editor should introduce and round off the book ('top and tail' it).
4 It should be in a field or an area where the presentation of, and comparison and contrast between, *different perspectives* or points of view will be of value and interest.
5 The authors should focus on the same set of themes and issues, preferably following a common format, with similar word limits.
6 Each chapter should also be similar in writing style, tone, vocabulary and level of readability; contributors should all be aiming at the same target audience or readership.

FROM THE PUBLISHER'S PERSPECTIVE

What happens inside the premises and the minds of publishers? How do they make decisions, and how has the process changed in recent years, if at all? How might the process change in the near future?

The decision-making process: another black hole?

The decision-making process with book publishers is in some ways similar to the process with journals in that both seem to involve a mixture of explicit and implicit criteria. However, there is one major difference: book publishers, and the people involved in making decisions on what and what not to publish, i.e. the commissioning editors, are very much in the business of making profits. It is true that journals also need to make money to stay afloat, but the nature of the people involved and their motives are different in many ways. For example, the editor of an academic journal and the journal's referees are usually working either for nothing (except professional satisfaction and development) or for a small honorarium and one or two small perks, e.g. a free copy of the journal. Journals would like to have 500 subscribers or more, but many survive with a relatively small readership, perhaps under 200. If book publishers consistently produced titles that sold only a few hundred copies they would soon cease to be in business. As Smedley (1993: 124) puts it, from an American context, 'Publishing is not a charitable venture . . . Publishing is a business and your book is a product to be sold to the appropriate customer . . . the bottom line, as with any other business, is that your book has to sell. If too many products don't sell, the publisher will be out of business.'

Commercial concerns are important – but decisions are not made on this criterion alone, as Walter Powell (1985) showed. Powell's ethnographic study included a fascinating insight into what he called 'the decision-making process in scholarly publishing'. He spent considerable time in two publishing houses in the USA, observing, talking with editors and shadowing them. His findings are worth considering at some length.

One of the publishers received 4,680 proposals in two years and accepted 140 of them (3 per cent). Another publisher from whom he obtained data received 1,321 in one year, and accepted 71 (5 per cent). Clearly, rejection rates are far higher than for even the most selective journal. So how did these commissioning editors actually make the decision to reject or (in the very rare cases) go through with a proposal? Powell comments that 'scholarly editors tend to get mystical when asked how they make their decisions'; they talk of 'skills that cannot be taught' or 'going with their sense of smell'. And yet in some ways they were able to make explicit many of their reasons for rejecting proposals. The major ones given were: the proposal is outside the competence or interests of the house (it doesn't 'fit the list'); there are too many books in that area already, and the publisher wishes to keep the list balanced; the proposed book covers the same ground as one in print or in the pipeline; the proposal is too demanding of the editor's time and energy ('it will create more work than they can handle').

Some of the grounds for rejection were directly related to the author: the author had 'proved to be cantankerous in the past'; the author's status and demands had risen to a level where the house could no longer afford him; or the editor could not understand the author's writing – it was too dense and complex, too abstract and theoretical.

In Powell's study some editors would accept a proposal even if that particular book was not likely to make money: the book might be good for PR, for the publisher's status, for keeping a good author happy, or for luring other authors to that publisher (bait). Exceptional books, though unlikely to be huge sellers, were sometimes accepted for adding what Bourdieu (1977: 177–183) called 'symbolic capital'. One editor in Powell's study said in conversation about a book that looked very novel and different: 'you just have to publish books like that one. I doubt we've made a penny on it, but I wouldn't hesitate to do it again. I personally enjoyed reading it. Besides books like that don't cost that much and they are worth doing' (Powell, 1985: 85). Publishers tell me that such practices are very unlikely to occur now, with profit being the overriding motive.

Powell's study showed the degree of power and freedom that commissioning editors then had when compared with their journal counterparts. My own current experience with book publishers partially resonates with Powell's study.

He commented that although editors almost always send proposals out to reviewers in the field, they may 'overlook unfavourable reviews'; 'they are given a substantial amount of rope' (p. 160). This was evident to me when I received feedback on the proposal for this book from three reviewers. The evaluations were, to use a euphemism, variable. One of them was even quite scathing. But the editor still worked through the proposal with me, suggesting some revision, and eventually offered me a contract to do what I am doing now. However, it must be noted that all editors in commercial firms have to seek approval from a committee in the organization, which sits regularly to consider book proposals formally. The committee is made up of senior editorial, marketing and sales staff, and I am told by one editor that 'getting a book through a meeting can be a pretty formidable process, so we need to be 100% confident about projects before going this far' (personal correspondence).

Editor behaviour

Powell's 1985 study was fascinating in that he closely observed what editors actually did. As already mentioned, they do spend a lot of valuable time networking – Powell described these 'informal circles' as a necessity, not a luxury.

Another observation concerned how editors actually allocate their time in considering proposals. They need strategies to cope with information overload. One editor coped with this by having two types of proposal in the 'queue': lowly regarded and highly regarded. This editor stated: 'If I were to give every manuscript equal attention, they would each get a three minute glance' (p. 227). One worrying but important observation made by Powell is that editors do take considerable notice of authors' status, and that of their employing organization, in allocating time and considering proposals. This is not the sole criterion, but it is a large one. Powell describes this as the 'Matthew Effect': 'Unto every one that hath shall be given' (from Matthew's gospel; and Merton, 1968 and Zuckerman, 1970 talked in a similar vein of the rich getting richer and the poor getting poorer). This effect 'serves to penalise the young and unknown' (p. 178). It is also linked to the importance of networks and informal circles. The institutions with the highest prestige and status also seem to have better connections, ties, networking, contacts, visibility and familiarity with editors in major publishing houses. In addition Powell comments that 'scholars employed at elite colleges and Universities have better facilities, greater research support, more release time and lighter teaching loads' (p. 179).

Book publishing: past trends and future predictions

This section considers the future of books from two very different perspectives: the author's and the publisher's. In 1997, Nixon carried out a study on the changing priorities in educational publishing by contacting all the major UK publishing outlets. Nixon's paper (1999) raised some fascinating issues about who was writing books and who was reading them. It raised questions about 'market imperatives'. Should authors be driven by market forces and respond to the demands and expectations of existing and developing audiences, or should they try to 'create their own audience' (Bourdieu, 1998)? If they try to achieve the latter, one might ask, will they ever get published?

Nixon's paper, with its data from the major publishers and its fascinating discussion of writing and reading in the education sphere, is worth reading in full. With his permission, I used a framework similar to his 1997 questionnaire and sent it by e-mail to seven major publishers at the end of 2002, i.e. five years on. Publishers were asked for their views on what makes a good author and a good book, how publishing has changed, and what the main influences on book publishing are, and will be. All responded, some writing extensively. There is insufficient space to include their responses verbatim here, but it should be useful to readers to summarize some of the key points emerging, many of which relate to Nixon's earlier study. Firstly, several useful practical points emerged from the question what makes a good author and a good book. For example, a 'good author' was variously described as one who delivers on time, writes to the agreed length, helps to market the book, and has the general qualities of being organized and communicative. A good author was also said to have a clear idea of what they want to say, the ability to write well and concisely, an awareness of the audience, and the ability to take care with presentation. A good book was said to be clear, coherent, relevant and well written and to carry a worthwhile message in a new and interesting fashion. A good book will have a very clear focus on who the book is for and who will read it.

Responses showed that the people writing books are often drawn from occupational groups very different from those who read them. Lecturers in HE, for example, may be writing books for practitioners in other phases and stages of education. Publishers are trying to meet the needs of the readership groups, which are becoming more focused, more utilitarian and more determined by central policies and initiatives. Thus most publishers felt that there is little scope for monographs or books arising from Ph.D. theses nowadays, unless they can really bring out the implications of their findings. One publisher described their 'mantra' as 'practical and accessible'.

This imperative is sometimes in direct conflict with the needs of, and pressures upon, those who are doing the writing. Publishers are producing books largely (though not exclusively) for profit and therefore aimed at as wide a readership as possible. For example, books on education are often targeted at teachers or lecturers, and students – rather than peers or fellow-researchers in a field. As a result, such books may not be judged to be reporting so-called 'state-of-the-art' or 'cutting-edge' research. The difficult task for the writer is to produce a book which is research based and underpinned by existing theory and literature, but is also of value to its readers and of interest to publishers. Without the underpinning foundation of research, theory and literature base the book's value in RAE currency may be deemed to be limited. Without a satisfactory market, its appeal to a commercial publisher will be insufficient to gain a contract.

What lies in the future for education book publishing? Clearly, if authors work in an environment where Research Assessment Exercises dominate, they will need to produce books that address the tensions between the needs of publishers, readers and Research Assessment Exercises – and it is not an easy task either to write the proposal to win the contract or to write the book itself. It seems that monographs, 'academic tomes', edited collections, and converted dissertations will become harder to get published commercially. A pessimistic view (that I don't share) is that there may be fewer possibilities for experiment and creativity in book writing. However, books look set to continue as a medium for publishing (an issue discussed in the last chapter) – but other media, or at least links to other media such as websites, must come into the writer's repertoire and the publisher's output.

Chapter 6

Practical guidance on writing

There is no shortage of guidance on writing and the writing process. This chapter selectively considers some of that guidance and attempts to distil the main points. The interview responses in Chapter 3 show that all writers are different. So there can be no set of handy hints or infallible guidelines which apply to all writers; different people will extract, from the wide range of guidance, the suggestions and claims that may work for them. The main message of the chapter is this: there is no one right way to write.

Classical models of writing and their dangers

The traditional, popular model of writing was based on the idea that 'what you want to say and how you say it in words are two quite separate matters' (Thomas, 1987). Others have called it the 'think and then write paradigm' (Moxley, 1997: 6); we do all of our thinking before we start writing. Elbow (1973) is, like Moxley and Thomas, a critic of the so-called classical model, and he sums up the view as follows:

> In order to form a good style, the primary rule and condition is not to attempt to express ourselves in language before we thoroughly know our meaning. When a man [sic] perfectly understands himself, appropriate diction will generally be at his command either in writing or speaking.

Thomas (1987: 95–98) analyses several ways in which a belief in this classical model can be harmful, or 'lead to trouble', as he puts it. Firstly, belief in the model creates the expectation that writing should be easy if 'you know your stuff'. Then, when people find it difficult (as they should – see p. 8), feelings of inadequacy and frustration set in. Secondly, the model leads to the implicit and incorrect belief that thorough knowledge will lead to clear, high-quality writing. This is not always true and can again lead to negative feelings. Thirdly, the expectation that writing is a linear process can lead to feelings of inadequacy and frustration as soon as the writer realizes that it is in fact recursive or cyclical. Finally, the classical model goes something like (in my words): do all your reading, grasp all your material, think it through, plan it out, then write. Writers who followed this would never get started.

In reality, as we saw in Chapter 3, thinking and writing interact. Thinking occurs during writing, *as* we write, not before it. Plans are a starting point for writers. Although a few writers follow them meticulously, most treat the plan as something to deviate from. Elbow (1973) described this model, the generative model, as involving two processes: growing and cooking. Writing various drafts and getting them on paper is growing; rereading them, asking for comments from others and revising is part of the cooking process. Adopting and believing in this 'generative model' (Thomas, 1987) will lead to several important attitudes and strategies, which I sum up as follows:

- Greater willingness to revise one's writing (drafting and redrafting)
- A willingness to postpone the sequencing and planning of one's writing until one is into the writing process (it is easier to arrange and structure ideas and words once they are out there on paper than if they are in our heads)
- A habit of 'write first, edit later'
- The attitude that extensive revisions to a piece of writing are a strength, not a weakness
- More willingness to ask for comment and feedback, and to take this on board
- Greater sensitivity to readers and their needs, their experience and knowledge and their reasons for reading your work.

In fact, writing is a form of thinking – it is not something that follows thought but goes along in tandem with it (Wolcott, 1990). Laurel Richardson (1990 and 1998) often describes writing as a way of 'knowing', a method of *discovery* and analysis. Becker (1986: 17) puts it beautifully by saying: 'The first draft is for discovery, not for presentation.' This process of learning, discovery and analysis does not precede the writing process – it is part of it. She tells of how she was taught, as many of us were, not to write until she knew what she wanted to say and she had organized and outlined her points. This model of writing has 'serious problems': it represents the social world as static and it 'ignores the role of writing as a dynamic, creative process' (Richardson, 1998: 34). Most harmful, for new writers, is that the model undermines their confidence and acts as a block or obstacle in getting started on a piece of writing. If we feel that we can't start until we know exactly what we think, what we intend to write and how we are going to organize it, then we will never get started. This is one of the reasons why Richardson objects to the term 'writing up' of research, as if it comes afterwards. Like the linear model of writing, this is based on a linear model of the research process, which puts 'writing up' as the last task (discussed fully in Wellington, 2000: 46–49). Over forty years ago, the Nobel prize-winning scientist Sir Peter Medawar (1963 and 1979) argued that virtually all scientists write up their research as if it were a clean, linear, non-messy, carefully planned process. In reality the process is far more messy and cyclical, hence Medawar's accusation that the typical 'scientific paper is a fraud'. Incidentally, he described the scientific method as a mixture of 'guesswork and checkwork' (1979), a process not unlike educational research.

Perhaps the main thing to remember about writing is that it is hard work. It is a struggle. It is difficult and can make your brain hurt. Writing clearly and succinctly is even more difficult. Having extensive experience of writing does not make it easier: it simply makes the writer more confident. In discussing the question of 'what people need to know about writing in order to write in their jobs', Davies and Birbili (2000: 444) sum up by saying: 'We would suggest that the most important kind of conceptual knowledge about writing should be, in fact, that in order to be good it must be difficult.'

Getting started

> The last thing one knows in constructing a work is what to put first.
> (Blaise Pascal, 1623–1662, French mathematician who put forward the idea of black holes)

Starting a piece of writing is the hardest thing to do, except perhaps for finishing it (or at least knowing when to stop – as Day, 1996, puts it: 'Papers can be completed, but the perfect paper cannot be'). Getting started on a piece of writing usually involves a kind of build-up to it: various authors have called this cranking-up, psyching up, mulling, organizing and so on (see Wolcott, 1990: 13 and Woods, 1999). One of the ways of building up is to read widely (and in my case, making notes on it, distilling thoughts and jotting down my own ideas and viewpoints). The problem, of course, lies in knowing when to stop reading and to start writing. My feeling is that initial reading is needed to help in the build-up process (cranking and psyching up) but that one should start writing before finishing reading – mainly because, in a sense, the reading can never stop. Reading should be done in parallel with writing ('in tandem', as Wolcott, 1990: 21, puts it). The two activities need to be balanced, with reading being on the heavier side of the see-saw initially and writing gradually taking over. Wolcott's view is that writing is a form of thinking and therefore 'you cannot begin writing early enough'.

Ideally, the writer reaches a point where their own writing is just waiting to get out there, onto the page. A kind of saturation point is reached. It starts to ooze out. As one of the interviewees said in Chapter 3, the iceberg breaks away. After that, I find that the whole thing is easier to keep moving – to carry on the metaphor, and mix it a little, it's as if the iceberg is gaining momentum.

This is the time when we should spend more time writing than we do reading – the balance shifts to the other side. I find at that stage that I can't wait to get back to writing. But even then, most of us engage in all sorts of displacement activities. My favourite, if I am writing at home, is to hoover the hall carpet. Dogs that like walking are another useful source of displacement. Computers can be valuable here too. Tidying up the hard disk or checking the e-mails as they come in can be an excellent distraction.

Finding time to write – or creating it

Dorothea Brande (1983) in her classic book, first published in 1934, suggests that a beginning writer should start off by writing for a set period at the same time every day. Once this discipline becomes a habit she suggests that you can write at a different time each day, provided you always set yourself an exact time and keep to it. Personally, I find this advice too rigid and impossible to adhere to if one has a busy and unpredictable working day or a complicated home life (as most people now have, even if they did not in 1934). Brande tends to use a physical education (PE) analogy for writing, talking of exercise, training oneself to write, using unused muscles and the value of early-morning writing. The PE analogy can be useful up to a point (it can be helpful to think of keeping in trim, exercising our writing muscles and taking regular practice), but perhaps should not be over-stretched.

One of the great dangers preventing us from finding or creating time to write is the tendency to wait for a big chunk of time to come along when we can 'really get down to it'. People convince themselves that productive writing will happen when they have a large block of uninterrupted time. This is one of the most common forms of procrastination: 'I'll just wait for that day, that weekend, that holiday or that period of study leave and then I can really get some writing done.' Boice (1997: 21) calls this the 'elusive search for large blocks of time. First colleagues wait for intersession breaks. Then sabbaticals. Then retirements.'

Haynes (2001: 12) suggests adopting simple routines for the beginning and end of each session. For example, one could begin with a 'freewriting' session of four or five minutes, just bashing out some words and sentences without pausing for correction, revision and certainly not editing. Haynes recounts that he likes to start a new writing session by making revisions to the text that he produced in the last one – a kind of warming-up exercise. He also suggests the ploy of finishing a writing session before you have written everything you want to write, with the aim of making you look forward to the next session. Some writers, he claims, actually end a session in the middle of a paragraph or even a sentence. Again, I'm not sure about this advice – I would be worried that I wouldn't know how to 'pick it up' again, or that I'd forget the plot completely, or that by stopping suddenly I might lose some useful words that were just about to come out!

Abby Day (1996: 114–115) suggests that one should limit any writing session to a maximum of two hours. After that, one should take a break, perhaps have a walk or a coffee and come back to it feeling refreshed. This is also good health advice if you are working in front of a screen – most safety guidance suggests short breaks at frequent intervals away from the screen, standing up and looking at distant objects to rest the eyes and neck.

Day offers no sympathy for those who say that they cannot find any time at all for a short writing session over a period of several days and do not organize their time:

> I always cringe when I read the acknowledgement section of a book or thesis and find sentences that apologize to the author's friends, family and children for being such a terrible person for the past weeks, months or even years. Doesn't the author know how to organize himself or herself? Good work is done in manageable portions. Getting out of bed an hour earlier or locking the office door for two hours now and then isn't too much to ask. Staring into space and panicking about how to start is a miserable, and largely ineffective, way to spend one's time.
>
> (Day, 1996: 115)

Different ploys, different times of day, different starting strategies will work for different people. I think that the main general advice is to carve out some time to write when it suits your working and domestic day best, and your own 'best time'; and then try to write little and often, not hope for an entire day when you can work uninterrupted. This may never come, and anyway, I challenge anyone to write productively for an entire day – two or three hours, if you can find them, can yield as much good writing as a solid day that you look forward to with great expectations only to force yourself to write.

Productive writers, good days and bad days

I've written 1,467 words of this chapter today and feel that I'm ready for a break. In my view, this is an excellent day. I wish that there could be more like this.

It's the next day now. Hartley (1997) produced a useful summary based on his own research with Branthwaite (1989) into what makes a productive writer in the discipline of psychology. His eight points can be transferred to writing in other areas, although point 3 looks a little dated now. His view was that 'productive writers' exhibit the following strategies. They:

1   Make a rough plan (which they don't necessarily stick to).
2   Complete sections one at a time (however, they don't always do them in order).
3   Use a word processor.

4 Find quiet conditions in which to write and if possible write in the same place or places.
5 Set goals and targets for themselves to achieve.
6 Write frequently, doing small sections at a time, rather than in long 'binge sessions'.
7 Get colleagues and friends to comment on their early drafts.
8 Often collaborate with long-standing colleagues and trusted friends.

Haynes (2001: 11) offers an even shorter list of the 'qualities of productive writers'. From his experience as a commissioning editor, the productive writer:

- Seeks advice
- Shares drafts
- Writes regularly (little and often).

He feels that his last point is most important. He calculates that if a writer can produce 500 words in an hour and write for three hours a week, that makes 1,500 words and 75,000 words in a year – good by anyone's standards, considering that this book is less than 50,000 words in length. Mind, it's not every day that I can produce 500 good words in an hour.

Structuring writing

Sprent (1995: 3) uses the terms 'macrostyle' and 'microstyle'. The latter is concerned with style and structure at the level of words, sentences and paragraphs; while macrostyle is concerned with larger blocks and structures such as sections and chapters, and the use of tables and figures. This distinction can be useful in thinking about writing, and this section examines elements of both.

There is considerable debate about how much structure authors should include in writing a report, thesis, book or article. Here we consider structure at four levels: overall content; within chapters; paragraphing; and sentence level.

Headings, sub-headings, sub-sub-headings . . .

Headings are valuable signposts in guiding a reader through a text and maintaining their interest or concentration. But it is always difficult to decide how many *levels* of heading to use. It is essential to use some heading, even if it is just the book's title. Below that level, most writers would agree that chapter headings are essential. But after that, how many levels 'down' should writers go in structuring their writing?

Book editors always advise authors to be clear, when writing, about the level of heading they are using at any given time. Headings are then identified as level A, level B and level C, for instance; a different font or typeface is used for each level.

For example:

Level A: **CHAPTER HEADINGS** (upper case, bold)
Level B: **Sub-headings** (upper and lower case, bold)
Level C: ***Sub-sub-headings*** (upper and lower case, bold italics).

Writers then need to be (or at least try to be) clear and consistent about which headings they are using and why. If a writer goes 'below' level C this can be difficult. Writers, and readers, begin to flounder when they get past the sub-sub-level.

Chapter structure

Headings and sub-headings can help to structure a chapter and break it down into digestible chunks. But there is also a useful rule, followed by many writers, which can help to give a chapter a feeling of coherence or tightness. This rule suggests that a chapter should have three parts (unequal in size):

- A short introduction, explaining what the author is going to write about;
- The main body, presenting the substance of the chapter; and
- A concluding section, rounding off the chapter.

This overall pattern works well for many writers, and readers, especially in a thesis, a research report or an article. It is rather like the old advice about preaching: 'Tell them what you're going to say, then say it, and then tell them what you've just said.' For many types or genres of writing it works well and assists coherence. However, if overdone it can become tedious.

One other way of improving coherence is to write link sentences joining one paragraph to the next or linking chapters. For example, the last sentence (or paragraph) of a chapter could be a signal or an appetizer leading into the next.

Connecting phrases and sentences

One of the important devices in writing is the logical connective. Connectives are simply linking words and can be used to link ideas within a sentence, to link sentences or to link one paragraph to the next. Examples include: 'Firstly', 'Secondly', 'Thirdly', 'Finally'; also 'However', 'Nevertheless', 'Moreover', 'Interestingly', 'Furthermore', 'In addition', 'In conclusion', 'Thus', and so on.

Connectives can be valuable in maintaining a flow or a logical sequence in writing; but be warned – readers can suffer from an overdose if they are used too liberally, especially if the same one is used repeatedly. Ten 'howevers' on the same page can become wearing.

All the tactics and strategies summarized above have the same general aim: to improve clarity and communication. Table 6.1 gives a summary of four useful

Table 6.1 Four useful strategies in structuring writing

Strategy	Meaning	Examples
Signposting	Giving a map to the reader; outlining the structure and content of an article, book or chapter, i.e. structure statements	This chapter describes ... The first section discusses ... This paper is structured as follows ...
Framing	Indicating beginnings and endings of sections, topics, chapters	Firstly, ... Finally, ... To begin with ... This chapter ends with ... To conclude ...
Linking	Joining sentence to sentence, section to section, chapter to chapter ...	It follows that ... The next section goes on to ... As we saw in the last chapter ... Therefore ...
Focusing	Highlighting, emphasizing, reinforcing, key points	As mentioned earlier ... The central issue is ... Remember that ... It must be stressed that ...

strategies which can be used in writing, whether it be an article, a book, a thesis or a conference paper.

Signposting is particularly important. Haynes (2001: 104) gives excellent practical advice on the use of signposts. They should refer back to the previous chapter or section; they tell the reader what to expect; and they often pose a question or introduce a theme that the forthcoming section, paragraph or chapter is going to explore.

Paragraphing

Different writers and different readers see paragraphs in different ways. If you give different readers a page of prose without paragraphs and ask them to divide it into paragraphs, they are unlikely to break it down in exactly the same way. A paragraph should ideally contain just one main theme, concept or category – but concepts come from people, and people vary (Henson, 1999: 64). It is really up to the writer to make these partly arbitrary decisions on paragraphing. The main criterion is that each paragraph should centre on one idea: 'when the author progresses to a new idea, a new paragraph should be used' (Henson, 1999). But this is easier said than done, especially in the heat of the writing process. It takes practice, it is an art (Henson, 1999: 66), and personal preferences will vary from one writer to another (and between editor and author sometimes).

Henson gives some useful tips on paragraphing (pp. 37–38). He suggests that short paragraphs help the reader – the reader should be able to remember in one 'chunk' all the ideas contained in a paragraph. His rule of thumb is that half a side of double-spaced typed text is enough for most readers to retain. Henson also suggests that whilst reading through what you've written, you should see if each paragraph follows from and advances upon the ideas in previous paragraphs. If not, they should be reordered. This process, of course, is greatly helped by the cut-and-paste facility in word-processing programs.

Audiences and the writing process

Numerous authors give the following advice: have an audience in mind as you write, even a specific person 'in front of you'. Smedley (1993: 30), for example, writes: 'Fix an ideal reader in your mind – a bright student in one of your classes, a junior colleague to whom you wish to explain your ideas, your Dean – and write with that person in your mind's eye.' This is probably useful advice (though it would be difficult to write for the Dean, the bright student and the 'junior' colleague all at once). But the interviews reported in Chapter 3 do show that the constant presence of an audience in one's mind can be constraining and inhibiting as much as enhancing and liberating. Free writing, as Elbow (1973) calls it, can be a useful way of getting started and beginning to get things 'out there' onto paper. Simply writing for oneself, perhaps in a kind of diary or reflective journal, can be less daunting than trying to get every word out as if someone is reading it. It is rather like talking to yourself (when you can say what you want to) as opposed to talking to an audience.

Having said this, I do agree that all writing designed for publication in some form, and the subsequent shaping and editing, should be geared towards an audience. Free writing, with no one in mind, may be a way of getting started, gathering one's thoughts and in some cases freeing up writer's block, but ultimately published writing has to be aimed at an intended readership and a writer needs some vision or at least 'visualization' (Sprent, 1995) of this.

Getting it off the desk . . . gradually exposing your work and going public

Most experienced authors (perhaps not all) seem to express the view that seeking feedback and comment on one's own writing from another reader is essential. Reading your own work is important but is no substitute for reading by someone else, first a critical friend and later (if possible) an 'outsider' or even a member of the target audience. The writer's own tacit, implicit knowledge of what they wish to say makes it hard to identify the missing elements or steps in their own writing that are somewhere in 'the head' but have not made it out onto the paper. These may be missing episodes in an account or missing steps in an argument, so that the writer seems to jump to a conclusion without adequate premises. The Greek word 'ellipsis' (meaning 'cutting short') seems to sum up these omissions neatly. Readers can spot a writer's ellipses more readily than writers can spot their own. Readers can also identify sentences that are clumsy or simply don't read well or 'sound right'. It is also easier to spot long-windedness or repetition in someone else's writing than in your own.

It is worth leaving your writing 'to stand' for a few weeks before rereading it yourself, but the outside reader is essential too. Richardson (1990) talks of the value of 'getting early feedback' on your writing, perhaps by giving an 'in-progress' seminar or paper, or using some other public forum. Wolcott (1990: 46) suggests that reading your own words aloud to yourself can help, but even better, a friend or colleague (it would need to be a good one) could read them to you so that you could listen and concentrate on 'what has actually reached paper – the experience you are creating for others, out of your own experience'. When the reader stumbles or 'gasps for air' (as Wolcott puts it), it is time to 'get busy with the editing pencil'.

Examining tired and overworked metaphors

Many writers warn against the use of tired, hackneyed metaphors. But they are hard to avoid. Our spoken and written language is littered with them (oops! There goes another). As Lakoff and Johnson's (1980) excellent study points out, we live by them; they are the bread and butter of language (and another). Perhaps the best advice, given that we cannot live without them, is that we should at least be fully aware of them, careful in using them and sensitive to them. Richardson (1998) writes that using old, worn-out metaphors, 'although easy and comfortable, after a while invites stodginess and stiffness' (p. 362). Writers invite 'being ignored'. She suggests that people should examine the metaphors they use in writing (having first read Lakoff and Johnson's book) and reflect on what they are saying by using them. Could they find alternative metaphors? For example, instead of talking of a theory as a building, a frame-work, a structure or a foundation we could see theory as 'a tapestry' or as 'an illness' (p. 362). How are the everyday metaphors that you use shaping your writing and thinking?

Becker (1986: 84–89) writes scathingly of book reviewers (and, in my experience, referees for journals are similar) who say that 'a cutting edge seems lacking' or 'it tries to cover a huge terrain' (my own favourite cliché from referees and film critics is 'ultimately flawed', which is meaningless to me). Becker also criticizes the tired metaphors in research papers including 'growing body of literature', 'falling between two stools', 'conceptual straitjackets' and 'mining data' in order to 'tease out' or 'ferret' results. In editing, he advocates cutting (oops!) metaphors such as these, but not all metaphors. He suggests leaving metaphors that are being used 'seriously', with due care and attention. If the metaphor is explored and its ramifications are discussed, then include it, he advises. 'Tired' metaphors are not taken seriously or explored – they are no longer 'alive': 'a metaphor that works is still alive. Reading it shows you a new aspect of what you are reading about' (p. 86). Such metaphors only work if they are fresh and original enough to catch the reader's attention. The origin and true referent of a tired metaphor has long been forgotten. Becker (1986: 88) uses the example of the 'bottom line', the literal referent of which is the final line of an accountant's report that tells you exactly where you stand in credit or in debit; but this metaphor is widely misused to mean a final offer, a price someone will not lower or the last straw (that broke the camel's back, of course). The literal referent has long been forgotten.

I think the main point is that metaphors are a permanent fixture in our language (Lakoff and Johnson, 1980). They are impossible to avoid, so we should use them with care and attention.

Writing an abstract

One of the hardest things to produce when writing a paper, or in writing the introduction or 'appetizer' for a book chapter, is the abstract. Day (1996: 113) says that the good abstract should contain at least three things: a statement of the purpose of the piece; an outline of the argument and the methodology; and a summary of the conclusions. She argues elsewhere that reviewers of journals have two main concerns in refereeing a piece of writing: what is this paper about? And why does it matter? So in the abstract and the text itself, authors need to state their purpose, give the reader signposts (to show where it is going) and say why it is important. They also need to state how far it goes (its scope) and what its limitations are.

Editing, drafting and redrafting

> I spent all morning putting a comma in, and the afternoon taking it out again.
>
> (Attributed to Lord Byron, in Woodwark, 1992)

Most writers on writing seem to agree on one thing: do not try to edit and write at the same time (Smedley, 1993; Henson, 1999; Becker, 1986). Haynes (2001: 111) identifies two parts to the writing process: the compositional and the secretarial. In the first stage, writers should concentrate on getting words onto paper, generating text, trying to get the subject matter clear in their own minds and covering the ground. The secretarial stage involves sorting out the structure and layout, correcting things like spelling and punctuation and tinkering around with words and sentences. Haynes describes the first stage as 'writing for the writer', the second as 'writing for the reader'. This second stage is perhaps where the writer really needs to be aware of the intended audience; in the first stage, the writer can care far less about what anyone will think about it, and this slightly carefree attitude can encourage freer writing.

The act of editing can interfere with the activity of writing. Smedley (1993: 29) observes that 'when people first sit down to write, they begin a sentence and immediately take a dislike to the way it is worded and start again'. This is the editor interfering with the writer. Both are essential, but both should be kept in their places. 'The writer writes, the editor edits.' She suggests leaving the first draft for a day or a week and coming back to it with your editor's hat on this time. Editing involves seeing if it makes sense, feeling for how well it reads, asking if things could be put more neatly and succinctly and cutting unnecessary words. She argues, as several people do in my interviews in Chapter 3, for a number of drafts: 'Write without editing, then edit, then re-write without editing, then edit once again. When you exhaust your own critical eye as an editor, enlist the assistance of your spouse, your colleagues, your students, your trusted friends . . . and ask them to be brutal' (Smedley, 1993: 30).

Becker (1986), who has written the best book I have found on writing for social scientists, believes that writers can 'start by writing almost anything, any kind of a rough draft, no matter how crude and confused, and make something good out of it'.

I could call this the pottery model of writing – start by getting a nice big dollop of clay onto the working area and then set about moulding and shaping. This model may not work for everyone, though. Zinsser (1983: 97) talks of feeling that he writes rather like a bricklayer. His thoughts, expressed at the time by someone who had just discovered the value of the word processor, are worth seeing in full:

> My particular hang-up as a writer is that I have to get every paragraph as nearly right as possible before I go on to the next one. I'm like a bricklayer. I build very slowly, not adding a new row until I feel that the foundation is solid enough to hold up the house. I'm the exact opposite of the writer who dashes off his entire first draft, not caring how sloppy it looks or how badly it's written. His only objective at this early stage is to let his creative motor run the full course at full speed; repairs can always be made later. I envy this writer and would like to have his metabolism. But I'm stuck with the one I've got.

An interesting passage, but my suspicion is that he was exaggerating his affinity for this model, to make his point more strongly. I personally feel that productive writers are those who do treat their first draft as a draft, waiting for their own redrafting, comment from a colleague and further redrafting. Those who do not are less likely to welcome feedback from a critic who is a friend, or judgement and evaluation from a referee who is not.

Towards the final stages of editing and revising, a piece of advice given by Harry Wolcott (1990) seems very helpful. He tells of how the idea came to him when he was assembling a new wheelbarrow from a kit: 'Make sure all parts are properly in place before tightening.' Before you start tightening your writing, he argues:

> Take a look at how the whole thing is coming together. Do you have everything you need? And do you need everything you have?
>
> (p. 48)

His list of necessary parts includes a statement of our own viewpoints and opinions. We may prefer not to or simply not be willing to provide it, but he believes that this will be construed as a 'typical academic cop-out' – a failure to answer the question 'so what?'.

> We may prefer not to be pressed for our personal reactions and opinions, but we must be prepared to offer them. It is not unreasonable to expect researchers to have something to contribute as a result of their studied detachment and inquiry-oriented perspective.

I agree. People should be expected to voice their own views and draw out the 'so what?' implications after a long piece of research. They can do this with due modesty and deference to past literature and research, but without overdoing the usual statement of humility and inadequacy. Wolcott (1990: 69) even argues that a study of a single case should lead to some judgement and opinion. In answer to the sceptic who challenges 'What can we learn from one case?' Wolcott gives the answer 'All we can'.

Watching every word and sentence

> I have made this letter longer than usual because I lacked the time to make it short.
>
> (Blaise Pascal)

A good old-fashioned guide by Bett (1952) gives simple advice: 'the essence of style is the avoidance of (1) wind (2) obscurity. In your scientific writing be simple, accurate and interesting. Avoid like the plague "as to whether" and "having regard to", beloved of the drawers-up of legal documents. Avoid "tired" words. Avoid "slang"' (p. 18).

One of the old clichés, which is a tired one but does have some truth in it, is 'make every word work for a living'. Zinsser (1983: 98) offers one practical way of removing what he calls 'clutter'. He suggests reading the text and putting brackets round every word, phrase or sentence that 'was not doing some kind of work'. It may be a preposition that can be chopped out (as in 'free up', 'try out',' 'start up', 'report back'); it may be an adverb that is already in the verb (as in 'shout loudly' or 'clench tightly'); it may be an unnecessary adjective (as in 'green grass' or 'smooth marble'). Brackets could also be put round the kinds of qualifiers that academics and politicians tend to use, such as 'tend to', 'in a sense', 'so to speak', or 'in the present author's view' (the latter is also circumlocution). Entire sentences could be bracketed if they repeat something already said (unless it really needs reinforcing) or add irrelevant detail (too much information, perhaps). By bracketing the words or sentences as opposed to crossing them out, the reader/editor or writer can then see whether the text can really do without them – if so, then delete.

Incidentally, Zinsser (1983: 103) also emphasizes the value of short sentences. He talks of how, in writing his own book:

> I divided all troublesome long sentences into two short sentences, or even three. It always gave me great pleasure. Not only is it the fastest way for a writer to get out of a quagmire that there seems no getting out of; I also like short sentences for their own sake. There's almost no more beautiful sight than a simple declarative sentence.

Haynes (2001: 93–96) gives excellent and witty advice on circumlocution. He identifies common examples such as 'at this moment in time' (meaning 'now'), 'until such time as' (meaning 'until'), 'is supportive of' (meaning 'supports') and 'is protective of' (meaning 'protects'). He suggests that two common causes of circumlocution are the use of euphemisms (e.g. 'going to meet their maker' instead of 'dying') and *pomposity*. There is no shortage of the latter in academic writing. Authors may attempt to impress their audience with a pompous tone and choice of words. They perhaps hope to appear knowledgeable and 'academic'. The end result is often the use of inappropriate and pretentious language. I am particularly wary of words such as epistemology, ontology, positivism, and most other -isms and -ologies. They are sometimes included in sentences which are meaningless. Haynes suggests that this may happen when authors 'feel superior to their audience', but also occurs when 'authors feel insecure either because they are short of material or they do not have a secure grasp of the subject' (p. 94). It is certainly something for both readers and writers to beware of. Every sentence, in a book or article or thesis, should make sense.

To illustrate these points, Haynes uses an example of circumlocution produced by Sir Arthur Quiller-Couch in 1916. Here is his rearrangement of Hamlet's well-known soliloquy:

> To be, or the contrary? Whether the former or the latter be preferable would seem to admit of some difference of opinion; the answer in the present case being of an affirmative or of a negative character according as to whether one elects on the one hand to mentally suffer the disfavour

of fortune, albeit in an extreme degree, or on the other to boldly envisage adverse conditions in the prospect of eventually bringing them to conclusion.

(Cited in Haynes, 2001: 94)

Shakespeare put it rather more neatly:

> To be, or not to be, that is the question:
> Whether 'tis nobler in the mind to suffer
> The slings and arrows of outrageous fortune,
> Or to take arms against a sea of troubles,
> And by opposing end them.

(*Hamlet*, Act III, Scene ii)

Checking your typing

Spellcheckers are marvellous things but they need to be handled with care:

> Owed to spell checkers
>
> I have a spelling checker
> I disk covered four my PC.
> It plane lee marks four my revue
> Miss steaks aye can knot see.
>
> Eye ran this poem threw it.
> Your sure real glad two no.
> Its very polished in its weigh,
> My checker tolled me sew.

(Original source unknown)

Spellcheckers are no substitute for human readers, especially if the human is *not* the writer. In my experience of writing and reading, the five most common areas where vigilant checking is needed are:

1   Missing apostrophes, e.g. 'The pupils book was a complete mess. Its true to say that apostrophes are a problem.'
2   Unwanted apostrophes, e.g. 'It's bone was a source of amusement.' (The use of 'it's' for 'its', and vice versa, is a common mistake.)
3   Referencing: referring to items in the text which are not listed in the list of references at the end, and vice versa, i.e. listing references which are not included in the text.
4   Commonly misused words: effect/affect; criterion/criteria; phenomenon/phenomena; their/there.

5   Sentences that don't make sense. There is a danger, particularly for new
    writers who are striving to show that they have been initiated into academic
    discourse, of 'shooting from the hip' with newly acquired buzz words. Jargon
    can be valuable; terms such as 'ontology', 'epistemology', 'paradigm', 'tri-
    angulation' and 'validity' can all refer to important concepts, but they can
    easily be strung together to form a grammatical but totally meaningless
    sentence. Here is an example that I constructed:

> The elusive epistemology of Smith's ambiguous ontology results in a
> problematic contestation of the discourse of reflexive dialectic, hybridiz-
> ing the hermeneutic parameters of discursive dialogue and transgressing
> the shifting boundaries of hegemonic signifiers.

In writing for publication, of course, the author has the added benefit of a copy-
editor and often a proofreader to check the text. But this does not relieve the
author (and their critical friend) of the responsibility of submitting as near
perfect an article, book proposal, sample chapter or typescript as possible.
Presentation is no substitute for substance, but it is a *necessary* prerequisite for
a positive reception (though not a *sufficient* one). Many editors suggest checking
your work from the bottom upwards, to avoid getting carried away by the
content and flow of the text you are reading. Many people talk of testing your
written sentences by ear: how do they sound and feel? Read aloud, read upwards
from the bottom, line by line.

'Good writers' and good writing

Really good writing is easier to recognize than to analyse. It is easier to identify
good writing than to define it. Equally, one person's idea of good writing may
not agree with another's. Here, I have singled out three authors (of non-fiction)
who, in my view, produce excellent writing.

(1) Firstly, Dava Sobel (1996) in her bestselling story *Longitude*: here, she
introduces the idea and explains why the development of a reliable clock was
so vital in the early eighteenth century:

> Here lies the real, hard-core difference between latitude and longitude –
> beyond the superficial difference in line direction that any child can see:
> The zero-degree parallel of latitude is fixed by the laws of nature, while
> the zero-degree meridian of longitude shifts like the sands of time. This
> difference makes finding latitude child's play, and turns the determination
> of longitude, especially at sea, into an adult dilemma – one that stumped
> the wisest minds of the world for the better part of human history.
>
> Precise knowledge of the hour in two different places at once – a longi-
> tude prerequisite so easily accessible today from any pair of cheap wrist-
> watches – was utterly unattainable up to and including the era of

pendulum clocks. On the deck of a rolling ship, such clocks would slow down, or speed up, or stop running altogether.

(pp. 4–5)

Sobel's punctuation may be unorthodox, but she has the knack of holding the reader's attention, clarifying difficult concepts and making a potentially dull account into a fascinating story.

(2) From a completely different field, Terry Eagleton is often praised for his incisive, original writing and thinking. Here, he explains how values and knowledge are inextricably linked:

Interests are *constitutive* of our knowledge, not merely prejudices which imperil it. The claim that knowledge should be 'value-free' is itself a value-judgement.

It may well be that a liking for bananas is a merely private matter, though this is in fact questionable. A thorough analysis of my tastes in food would probably reveal how deeply relevant they are to certain forma- tive experiences in early childhood, to my relations with my parents and siblings and to a good many other cultural factors which are quite as social and 'non-subjective' as railway stations. This is even more true of that fundamental structure of beliefs and interests which I am born into as a member of a particular society, such as the belief that I should try to keep in good health, that differences of sexual role are rooted in human biology or that human beings are more important than crocodiles. We may disagree on this or that, but we can only do so because we share certain 'deep' ways of seeing and valuing which are bound up with our social life, and which could not be changed without transforming that life.

(Eagleton, 1983: 14)

Later he states:

The largely concealed structure of values which informs and underlies our factual statements is part of what is meant by 'ideology'.

(3) Finally, another author who succeeds in putting across difficult concepts in a lucid, accessible way is the geneticist Steve Jones. In his 1996 book *In the Blood*, he discussed genetics, evolution and inheritance. One of his special knacks is to tease out all sorts of paradoxes and contradictions:

At first sight, evolution has got it wrong. If humans followed the rules that apply to other animals, Europeans ought to be black and Africans white. Most creatures from hot sunny places are not dark but light, for the simple reason that black objects absorb more of the sun's heat. A black person in sunlight absorbs a third more solar energy than does someone with white skin.

Humans are tropical animals, which explains why most people wear clothes most of the time. Give people from the Equator or the Poles the choice and they set the central heating at the same level. Cold is dangerous. The blood gets sticky, veins contract and blood pressure goes up. All this makes the heart work harder. Deaths due to heart disease and stroke show a dramatic increase – by one-tenth for every three-degree drop in temperature – in chilly weather. In the British midwinter, the number of strokes is twice that during the summer. Even a cool rather than a comfortable living-room increases the risk of death. This alone explains why the increase in winter death rate is twice as great among poor people than among rich. Anything that helps people from cold places to warm up (black skin included) should, it seems, be favoured.
(Jones, 1996: 190)

These are three examples of what I would consider to be good writing. I won't try to pick out the common characteristics, especially as they all write so differently. But three of the features which, for me, make their writing good are: the mixture of sentences of different length and style; the ability to surprise, to grab the reader's attention and to keep it; and the use of concrete, familiar examples on which to pin difficult concepts. (Eagleton talks of a 'liking for bananas', Sobel mentions 'cheap wristwatches' and Jones writes of 'black skin' and 'sticky blood'.)

Woods (1999) provides an excellent discussion of what he calls successful writing. One of his criteria for good writing is what he calls 'attention to detail'. He quotes the novelist David Lodge, who describes how he learnt to 'use a few selected details, heightened by metaphor and simile, to evoke character or the sense of place' (p. 13). This art, or craft, is equally useful in writing on education. Woods also talks of the importance of being able to express these in writing. The ability to connect or synthesize ideas is actually an aspect of creativity which sometimes shows itself in educational writing and research. It might be the ability to connect and interrelate one's own findings with existing research or theory, it might be a synthesis of ideas from two completely different domains of knowledge, e.g. using literature from a seemingly unrelated area, or it might be the application of a theory or model from one field to a totally new area. Syntheses or connections of this kind can be risky, and require a degree of self-confidence, but made well they can be illuminating.

In discussing the writing up of qualitative research, Woods (1999: 54–56) also talks of the importance of including 'other voices' in the text, besides that of the author. One of the objectives of educational research is to give people (teachers, students, pupils, parents) a voice or a platform, and this must be reflected in the written medium through which the research is made public. Giving people a voice, however, leads to some difficult choices. Every write-up is finite. Do you include lengthy statements or transcripts from one or two people, or many shorter points from a larger variety? (See Woods, 1999: 56 for discussion.)

A final point made by Woods concerns the importance, when writing, of not missing the humorous side of research, e.g. by including an ironic comment from an interviewee.

A large body of research has been published on the differences between 'good' and 'poor' writers, some of which we looked at in Chapter 3. The most commonly cited authors are Flower and Hayes. Their 1981 work, for example, concluded that good writers engage in 'global planning' that incorporates rhetorical concerns such as audience, purpose and intention. So-called 'poor writers' engage in local planning, focusing on surface features of their writing. Of course, empirical evidence to support these distinctions (and for the models presented earlier) is hard to obtain. How can a researcher actually observe writers, and their minds, at work?

Humes (1983) provided an interesting review of the different methodologies used to study the writing process. She reports a variety of methods ranging from: laboratory studies of writers (observed either by a person in the same room or through a one-way screen); naturalistic studies of writers in their usual settings, either observed or video-taped; studies of writers' products, such as drafts, revisions of drafts, jottings or notes; and even scans of writers' brains during writing. Her research review adds further support for the recursive model of writing discussed at the start of this chapter. In fact, writers move back and forth between the different sub-processes of writing, planning, thinking, composing, translating into words – they move from one to the other during writing, as opposed to following a linear path. Humes (1983) argued that different types of writing require different amounts of time, planning and pauses: e.g. generalizing and discussing needs more time than reporting.

Subsequent researchers have even studied physical activity in certain muscles in the region of the mouth and larynx, on the assumption that this corresponds with mental activity. A body of research has studied these muscular responses (calling them 'covert linguistic behaviour'). One study (Williams, 1987) even argued that 'below-average' writers exhibited much less covert linguistic behaviour during *pauses* in writing than those deemed to be 'above-average'. During these pauses, it is argued, the good writers are engaged in the global planning and thinking mentioned earlier. I can't say that I'm convinced by these inferences from muscle twitches, but perhaps I need to observe some busy writers closely.

Writing the 'other bits', especially in books

Authors are usually asked to help with producing the jacket blurb for a book, provide some thoughts for the flyer, produce an index, write a preface and make the necessary acknowledgements. The latter can be particularly embarrassing. Wolcott (1990) satirizes the gushing, clichéd, thanking-God tributes that wonder how on Earth the spouse/children/dogs/cats/neighbours managed without the author while they slaved away on this book (probably a huge relief in most cases). Douglas Adams did a minor send-up of such acknowledgements by saying at the front of his *Hitch-Hiker's Guide to the Galaxy* that he was not married with three children, had no dogs or cats and did not live in Surrey.

Tools of the trade and sources of guidance

McCallum (1997) suggests that the two main tools for a writer are a 'big fat dictionary' and a good thesaurus. I agree. The best present I ever had was *The Shorter Oxford English Dictionary* (it comes in two large volumes). The writer also needs a good word processor and a healthily sized screen, although (see Chapter 3) some writers genuinely still prefer a pen and notepad for composing.

Other guides and sources of information can be useful, and many can be found on the World Wide Web. For example, the Publishers' Association have a helpful website, discussing a range of issues to do with publishing. They have four good pages on getting published, including advice on self-publishing and a warning about vanity publishing (www.publishers.org.uk). An equally valuable website is located at http://www.may.ie/nirsa/geo-pub/geo-pub.html. This was written primarily for geographers wishing to write and publish but is of value to authors in any field since it contains general advice on writing for journals, the refereeing process, dealing with copy-editing and proofreading and seven other sections on writing and disseminating work.

If you are seeking a publisher, AcqWeb's *Directory of Publishers and Vendors* can be valuable, especially the section that gives publishers' websites in a wide range of subject areas (http://acqweb.library.vanderbilt.edu). If you are seeking advice on English usage, see *The King's English* by H. W. Fowler, originally published by Clarendon Press in Oxford in 1908, now on the web through Bartleby of New York (www.bartleby.com). A paper equivalent (almost) is the *MHRA Style Book*, from the Modern Humanities Research Association in London. This is a guide of about eighty pages on style, spelling, referencing, indexing, proofreading – indeed almost anything to do with preparing articles, papers or books for publication. One specific issue that comes up frequently is e-referencing, i.e. referring to electronic sources. The best guide I have found on this comes from the University of Bournemouth. They have an excellent site on referencing in general with a good section on how to refer to e-journals, personal electronic communications, CD-ROMs, and so on (www.bournemouth. ac.uk/using_the_library).

A summary: some useful guidelines on writing

In this final section, I have collected together the fifteen pieces of advice on writing which I have found the most useful. They have been distilled from a variety of sources:

1   Don't procrastinate by waiting for the 'perfect opportunity' or the 'ideal writing conditions' such as a free day or a period of study leave before you start writing. They may never come.

2   Don't edit as you write, i.e. as you go along. Wait until later. Composing and revising/editing are different activities (like growing and cooking: Elbow, 1973).

3   Treat writing as a form of thinking. Writing does not proceed by having preset thoughts which are then transformed onto paper. Instead, thoughts are created and developed by the process of writing. Writing up your work is an excellent, albeit slightly painful, way of thinking through and making sense of what you have done or what you're doing. This is a good reason for not leaving writing until the end; writing should begin immediately.

4   Break a large piece of writing down into manageable chunks or pieces which will gradually fit together. I call this the 'jigsaw puzzle' approach – but an overall plan is still needed to fit all the pieces together. The pieces will also require linking together. The job of writing link sentences and link paragraphs joining section to section and chapter to chapter is vital for coherence and fluency.

5   Share your writing with a trusted friend – find a reader/colleague on whom you can rely to be reliable and just, but critical. Look for somebody else, perhaps someone with no expertise in the area, to read your writing and comment on it. They, and you, should ask: is it clear? Is it readable? Is it well structured? In other words, use other people, use books, e.g. style manuals, books on writing. Check your own typing, but always ask someone else to cast an eye over it too.

6   Draft and redraft; write and rewrite – and don't either expect or try to get it right first time. Writing should not be treated as a 'once and for all' activity. Getting the first draft onto paper is just the first stage. Then 'put it in the ice box and let it cool' (Delton, 1985).

7   Remove unnecessary words; make each word work for a living. After the first draft is on paper go back and check for excess baggage, i.e. redundant words and circumlocution.

8   Avoid tired and hackneyed metaphors.

9   Think carefully about when you should use the *active* voice in your sentences and when the *passive* voice may be appropriate. The passive voice can be a useful way of depersonalizing sentences, but sometimes naming the 'active agent' helps clarity and gives more information.

10 Be honest with your reader. Feel free to admit, in writing, that you found it hard to decide on the 'right way' to organize your material, decide on a structure, get started, write the conclusion, etc. Don't be afraid to say this in the text (Becker, 1986).

11 Vary sentence length. Use a few really short sentences now and again, say of four words. These can have impact.

12 Edit 'by ear'; make sure that it sounds right and feels right. Treat writing as somewhat like talking to someone except that now you are communicating through the written word. The reader only has what is on paper. Readers, unlike listeners, do not have body language, tone of voice or any knowledge of you, your background or your thoughts. Writers cannot make the assumptions and short cuts that can be made between talkers and listeners. Have your readers in mind, especially in the later stages of drafting. Better still, visualize one *particular* reader. What will they make of this sentence?

13 Readers need guidance, especially in a long article or book. In the early pages, brief the readers on what they are about to receive. Provide a map to help them navigate it.

14 Above all, get it 'out of the door' (Becker, 1986) for your friendly reader to look at. Don't sit on it for months, 'polishing' it. Get it off your desk, give it to someone to read, then work on it again when it comes back.

15 Finally, two of the most common obstacles to writing are (a) getting started and (b) writing the abstract and introduction. You can avoid the former by not trying to find the 'one right way' first time round (Becker, 1986), and the latter by leaving the introduction and abstract until last. Writing with a word processor helps to overcome both.

Chapter 7

Future publishing

Speculating on the future of any activity where technology is involved is a very uncertain science. Publishing is no exception. I would not dare to predict the future of book and journal publishing, but I know some authors who would, and have done. This chapter looks at a few possibilities.

Some of the clichés or 'yesterday's tomorrows'

Talk of the paperless office began in the 1970s. Can you see any evidence of this in your own workplace? My experience is that the volume of paper in most institutions seems to have increased by several orders of magnitude. Even the advent of the e-mail attachment has not reduced the amount of ambient paper in the workplace – in most cases, it has simply shifted the burden of printing it (or copying it) onto the receiver.

Past predictions of the future we face as a result of new technology include a good range of gaffes:

- IBM made fewer than twenty of their first model of computer. They thought that the world could not possibly cope with, or need, more.
- American experts forecast in 1955, when there were 250 computers in the USA, that the country would contain 5,000 by 1965. In fact, there were 20,000. By 1975 there were 80,000, quite large machines because the microcomputer had not arrived. Twenty million microcomputers were sold in the USA in 1979.
- In the late 1940s, British experts forecast that five of their new-fangled, giant machines would be enough for Britain's needs. Today, equally powerful computers can be carried in the palm of a hand.
- In 1948 George Orwell wrote his world-famous novel *Nineteen Eighty-four*. Everyone would be watched over by television cameras, and detailed information about everyone's beliefs, habits, likes and dislikes would be secretly stored by the ruling Party. 'Big brother' would be watching us. It seems now that Orwell was probably the most accurate.

Similarly, predictions of the 'end of the book' or the 'coming of the digital age' deserve some healthy scepticism. Future tellers have forecast a new style of reading, shifting from the traditional linear approach to a non-linear, hypertext model where the reader shifts constantly from one part of the text to another and back again. Yet the concept of hypertext is far from new. Some argue that it dates back to the creative thinking of Vannevar Bush in 1945, who suggested that we should be able to read as we think, i.e. non-sequentially and freely, but the term 'hypertext' was actually coined by Ted Nelson in 1965 (further discussion in N. Woodhead, 1991).

People can still read linearly (if they want to) or they can jump around, as many of us do, if that suits the text and their mood. All that new technology has done is perhaps to invite the reader to go into 'hyper-reading' mode and enabled hyper-links to be put into electronically readable text that either prompt the reader more obviously or speed up the jumping-around process. They also, one must admit, allow readers to jump readily (though not instantaneously, as some ICT zealots claim) from one source to another, by clicking a mouse button.

The journal: past and present

If we look back over the last few centuries it seems that different media for communicating knowledge have been present, and in some cases dominant, at different times. For example, one method of sharing and disseminating knowledge was correspondence between 'men of letters'. It occurred in the time of Boyle and Hobbes (on science in the seventeenth century), Leibniz and Newton (on mathematics and science in the late seventeenth and early eighteenth centuries), Kant and Hume (on philosophy in the nineteenth century), and Michael Faraday and other scientists such as Davy and Lord Kelvin in the early nineteenth century. Faraday and others in that era also disseminated their work through events at the Royal Institution, such as public lectures and demonstrations, or 'Friday evening discourses'.

Journals such as the *Philosophical Transactions of the Royal Society* (1664) were established in the seventeenth and eighteenth centuries. Indeed, journals in paper form have been around for several centuries (see Weiner, 2001). As journals gradually took over, the system of refereeing changed, and peers moved from being 'witnesses' to each other's work to being 'judges' of their peers' writing (see Larochelle and Desautels, 2002). But, like the correspondence between 'men of letters' and the events at the Royal Institution and other learned societies or bodies, journals of the past were hardly accessible, let alone universal. Now, in the twenty-first century, the market and audience for a journal are (in theory at least) global. As university presses and then commercial publishers became involved in 'the journal', their accessibility and readership widened. Their availability in electronic form further increased their readership and accessibility to a global audience. In theory, then, journals are now open to anyone to write for them and to read them. In practice, as we have seen in this book, getting an article published in a journal is considerably more complex. First of all, as discussed in Chapter 5, potential authors need to know the rules of engagement – the ground rules – before submitting to any journal. Weiner (2001: 4) calls this a 'social game, the rules of which need to be understood before individuals are able to successfully engage with it'. In addition, people involved in writing for and reading journals become a 'discourse community' (Weiner, 2001) with shared characteristics such as common aims, mechanisms for communicating with and informing each other, shared language practices and a required level of expertise and knowledge. These are fairly demanding requirements when you add them up – perhaps not as exclusive as in the days of 'men of letters', but not qualitatively different. Finally, certain people and groups still hold the ability to put the stamp of authority and approval (or not to, as the case may be) on the writing or the knowledge submitted to them. Journals control knowledge as well as disseminating it. As we saw in Chapters 4 and 5, although editors are sometimes reluctant to see themselves as gatekeepers, they do close doors as well as open them. Weiner in 2001 and in her earlier work with Packwood et al. (1997) describes this process as the *legitimation* of knowledge. The idea is based on the writing of Foucault (1980), who described how certain groups have the power to shape and control knowledge. Packwood et al. (1997: 5) argued that 'the more prestigious the journal, the more powerful the agent of legitimation'. Unofficial or amateurish knowledge may be excluded or disqualified as 'unrigorous, undisciplined, and unprofessional' (Agger, 1991: 41, cited by Packwood et al.).

So in this sense (of legitimating and excluding), journals and the way they operate have changed in degree but not in kind. This is one of the reasons why some individuals and groups have been arguing for change. In two other senses, journals *have* changed, and these changes have perhaps provided the main impetus for further evolution. The first change, over the last two or three decades, relates to increases in subscriptions, which seem to have come with commercialization of the journal. Many journals have been taken over by commercial publishers as opposed to (say) the university presses that were involved in the 1960s (Weiner, 2001). As my colleague Professor Tom Wilson pointed out in 2001, the raw material for journals comes free, and yet universities are paying more and more for it (he reported that the journals budget in the University of Sheffield was running at about £1 million per annum). Universities are buying back their own products. Indeed, I would argue that academic institutions are paying four times over: for the time taken to write the articles, for the time needed to referee and edit submissions, for the journals themselves (subscriptions have risen sharply) and for the time taken to read the articles. Weiner (2001) and others have argued that this trend towards commercialization of journals has led to far less feeling of 'belonging' amongst the community who write or referee for them and read them.

The second main change, which may be partly due to Research Assessment Exercises but is certainly due to the general pressure on people to publish more, is the proliferation of new journals. More and more journals are now published, some said to be of dubious quality.

The combination of commercialization and proliferation has led to huge burdens on libraries, which are fighting to keep up with the so-called 'knowledge explosion'. It has also led to rebellion amongst the ranks of normally placid academics (according to Glass, 1999). He reported that academics in several faculties in the USA were refusing to cede copyright of their work to commercial publishers and members of editorial boards were resigning in large numbers in order to create either free or at least low-cost alternatives to traditional journals. There are also increasing numbers of stories of authors who are boycotting journals that have imposed huge price rises, by not submitting to them. For example, a group was recently established with the name Scholarly Publishing and Academic Resources Coalition (leading to the neat acronym SPARC, website www.arl.org/sparc). SPARC was set up in response to the rapidly rising prices of journals with the aim of encouraging co-operation and sharing amongst colleagues. Others have talked of new models by which scholars can communicate with each other. Willinsky (2000), for example, writes of a 'Knowledge Exchange Model' (KEM) for publishing, which uses 'peer to peer communication at the institutional level of the research library'. The model cannot be considered in full here, but in short, rather than paying huge subscriptions to commercial publishers, libraries would redirect resources to building up and sustaining this 'knowledge exchange' and thereby provide 'free universal access to what is claimed to be a public good'.

In addition, scientists in particular have been undermining traditional peer review by saying: 'give me the article as soon as it's written. I can make up my own mind if it is right or not' (Glass, 1999). Drawing on his own experience of two electronic journals in education (*Education Policy Analysis Archives* and *Current Issues in Education*), Glass talks of a 'new day in how scholars communicate'. He talks of the new age of scholarly communications promising 'wide access at low cost'. In addition, by studying the daily access logs to articles, journal editors can see exactly who is reading the articles and where they come from. Such information can be gratifying as well as informative, Glass argues.

These changes will reshape what scholars mean by 'publication' as well as the very nature of their own work. The medium, I would add, could well shape the message and in turn the way that people write in the future. Writing may well be different for an entirely 'electronic audience', one might predict.

The electronic journal: pros and cons

Many journals now exist in two forms: print on paper and the electronic version. But Wilson and others wanted to take the evolution a stage further by making them entirely electronic. The main argument seems to have been cost related. If a group of people organize their own entirely electronic journal, then the costs (it is alleged) can be minimal. University staff, for example, will not be buying back their own products. I have collected together some of the other arguments for going entirely electronic and summarize them as follows:

1   Speed: the whole process, from submission through to refereeing to e-publication, will be speeded up. Submissions can be handled more quickly, as can communication with authors.
2   An electronic journal allows the use of media other than words and tables. It can use sound, video, digital photographs and so on: i.e. e-journals can use multimedia. Written text can be easily linked to multimedia.
3   Hypertext makes more flexible modes of reading possible.
4   There can be more interaction between writer and reader, and greater ease of communication.
5   There can be more inclusivity in who writes for the journal and whose papers are accepted, i.e. more equal opportunities for writers.
6   There will be wider distribution and dissemination, wider access to the journal and therefore a much wider readership worldwide.
7   Authors retain copyright in their own writing (which may not be the case with some journals).
8   Libraries can save huge amounts of shelf space by opting for the e-version only of a book or journal.
9   E-journals and e-books are more easily searched and annotated. Diction-aries and encyclopaedias are especially enhanced in their electronic form.
10 One final argument used by some is that the existing process of peer review and alleged 'gatekeeping' can be removed. Articles can be accepted pro-vided that they lie within the scope of the journal and they are acceptably presented and formatted. The choice of what to read will then lie with the reader.

These arguments in favour of the entirely electronic journal and its advantages are all highly contentious. For example, is there any reason why the refereeing process should be speeded up, especially when the novelty of e-journals has worn off? Flexible modes of reading are possible with traditional text. Inclusivity may or may not increase depending on how a journal is run and disseminated, who is involved in refereeing, and so on. Gatekeeping is equally possible in e-publishing and in print on paper. Searching is indeed easier with elec-tronic text – but it can throw up all sorts of red herrings and unwanted, useless results or 'hits' which 'human' searching and intuition would rule out. Libraries may save shelf space by not including print versions, but will they then be obliged to provide more computer facilities to access the e-version? The debate goes on.

A number of arguments have been marshalled against the solely electronic journal. Again, my summary follows:

1   It will encourage hasty and shoddy submissions by writers, which are of lower quality in content and presentation, e.g. badly checked for errors.
2   Access is only widened if the readers have access to ICT of the kind and the quality that enables them to read electronic documents.
3   Most people are willing to read short amounts of text from a screen, such as e-mails or mobile text messages. But few people are comfortable with reading several thousand words from a screen, e.g. a full journal article or a book chapter, let alone an entire book.
4   Reading from a screen for long periods is not good for the eyes or the neck muscles, for instance.
5   If, as a result of going electronic, a journal adopts more hasty and less stringent peer review, the quality will be lower.
6   Submissions, versions after revision, final drafts and proofs are harder to handle electronically and to monitor and keep track of (see editors' interviews in Chapter 4).
7   Archiving of electronic-only articles is far harder and more 'ephemeral' than of print-on-paper issues. The latter provide hard, physical copy as opposed to virtual storage, which may not be accessible in five years from now as technology changes (for example, my own Ph.D. in the 1980s was written on a 'BBC micro' using a word processor called Wordwise and stored on a very floppy five-inch disc that is not readable by any system currently in use).
8   The prestige of e-journals vis-à-vis print on paper will be far lower, or at least may be perceived to be by assessors in a Research Assessment Exercise.
9   Electronic journals provide far greater opportunities for plagiarism and for self-plagiarism, i.e. authors recycling their own work.

Again, there are many counter-arguments to these arguments. Why should e-journals have lower standards of peer review? Given time, why should the prestige of e-only journals not be as high as the prestige of those in traditional media? Why do e-journals and e-books make plagiarism more likely, when text can easily be scanned into a computer, or simply copied out as has always been the case? And as for self-plagiarism, what could be easier for an author who has a reasonably well-organized hard disc of past material?

The choice for the future, it seems, is between three options: commercially produced journals that offer both a print-on-paper and an e-version, at a price; electronic-only journals, but at a price; electronic journals that are open access (and at first sight apparently 'free' – except that the authors, editors and referees are likely to be paid by someone), i.e. they don't charge a subscription. It may be that these options will all survive, side by side.

Self-publishing, the future of peer review and the death of the referee

Earlier chapters have considered the nature of peer review, its proponents and its critics. What will happen to peer review as the nature of publishing changes?

In addition to the evolution of the journal it seems likely that the increase in self-publishing, e.g. via individuals' creation of their own websites, will continue without constraint. Similarly, other forms of freely available material will expand, e.g. by groups and societies making conference papers and proceedings freely available electronically. It may then be the case that new technology will simply overturn, usurp or render obsolete the centuries-old system of peer review. If authors are stopped from publishing what they want to, they will simply do so anyway, without any control or gatekeeping from their peers. Osborne and Brady (2002) argue that, if this movement continues, then the purpose of refereeing should be to encourage people to 'say things better' rather than to try to stop them. De facto (or post hoc) peer reviewing will then become the norm, i.e. some papers will be read and cited while others will just be ignored and wither away and die. The question for the future of this new form of peer review will then be: by which criteria will readers make their own decisions about what to read, to cite and therefore to 'keep alive'? Will they be just as mysterious, biased, uncivil and whimsical as the current system of peer review has been accused of being?

The book

Books, like journals, have been around for centuries. Like the arrival of the paperless office, the impending death of the print-on-paper book has been greatly exaggerated. In Britain, the number of original titles published in 2001 was 119,000 – this can be compared with a figure of 13,810 in 1927, i.e. roughly a ninefold increase. From 2001 to 2002, the number of books sold in the USA increased by 1.6 per cent to 557 million (data from Mundy, 2002). It is clear that books printed on paper are certain to continue, at least in the near future. Mundy (2002: 30) speculates that 'despite the e-book scare of a few years ago, paper is still going to be the primary means by which most works of fiction and non-fiction are published'. Later he writes:

> For the next decade or two, the paperback book will continue to be the most cost effective portable storage device ever invented.
>
> (Mundy, 2002: 30)

So what of the electronic book? Technology has developed in ICT, largely independently of the publishing industry. As Mundy (2002) puts it, publishers have had to watch and wait while technology has evolved. However:

Two of the pre-requisites for successful e-books are nearly upon us – improved battery power and display technology.

(Mundy, 2002: 30)

In the near future, most e-book devices will also have a voice function, enabling the text to be read out loud to the reader (listener) while in the car, bus, train or plane. (In some ways, this hardly seems an advance since a simple personal tape player can do this already with the 'audio book'.)

But there is also the aesthetic quality of paper books to consider. Many are pleasing to the senses – of touch, sight and smell. They make good presents and possessions, and are likely to retain their appeal whatever happens to the e-book, although (as Mundy, 2002, points out) there will be generational differences in preference, as with all technologies.

One of the major changes likely to result from e-publishing generally will stem from the huge potential it offers to authors at any level for *self-publishing*. Writers can now bypass the publisher and simply make their work available on the Internet. This can be true not only for the new author but also for the big names in writing such as Stephen King or Michael Crichton. By placing their latest novel on a website, for readers to download for a fee, they become their own publishers (Mundy, 2002). They simply need to buy in marketing, promotion and publicity. Similarly, academics can (and many do) have their own website and put their writing onto it. It may be available free of charge, or it may not. It might have been refereed and proofread, but not necessarily.

One major publisher of textbooks makes some interesting predictions on the future of books:

> I think you will see a multiplicity of media in the future, rather than one medium replacing another. If you look at the history of media in general, when a new medium comes along it does not usually replace an earlier one. It just adds to it.
>
> (Midgley, 2002)

Video did not kill radio. Haynes (2001: 150–163) presents some interesting views on the future of the 'textbook in the electronic age', and some of these points can be extended to other types of book and indeed journals. Several factors might lead to the decline of traditional books. The first is inevitably the high cost of books, especially set textbooks. Students, especially, will seek out lower-cost alternatives to paying out £20 or £30, such as Internet material or material 'placed on the Web' by a helpful lecturer (legally, it is hoped). A second factor likely to drive change is the advent of micropayments, for parts of a text. In buying a book, we purchase all or nothing. A digitized, electronic book can be bought by the section or passage – a reader can pay for and download only those parts of a book that they require. However, Haynes also points out some of the problems related to micropayments and the extraction of passages from full texts. For example, the reader would always be reading sections or passages out of context, not knowing where they fitted into a text or how they related to other areas. The economics of payment might also pose problems: would it be profitable for a publisher if students (especially) were paying for small chunks? How much would people be prepared to pay for extracts, and how would they choose these if they did not really know the entire text and context? Apparently, publishers are having considerable trouble in deciding on the right economic model for e-texts (see also Midgley, 2002).

Haynes (2001: 159–162) is one of the few people willing to stick his neck out and make specific forecasts on the future of books. He predicts that it will become commonplace ('de rigueur') for books to be supported with websites, hyperlinks and in some cases multimedia on one platform or another. Books will increasingly become available in dual format, i.e. as print on paper and as e-books. Customers can then choose between buying the whole thing or buying in parts through micropayments. Future changes will have interesting consequences for authors. Writers will need to take account of publishers' potential to work with electronic media and exploit their potential when they weigh up which one to submit work to. Similarly, authors being offered contracts will need to take far greater care in reading the section on electronic rights, considering not only the possible payments involved but also the extra work they may be loaded with, e.g. much more frequent updating of electronic texts, hyperlinks and websites.

In concluding . . .

A safe forecast is that the whole nature of publishing, quality control and peer review is set to change. Mundy sees a bright future for authors and readers but a less certain time for publishers:

> The future, it seems, belongs to writers, readers and entrepreneurs. There will be as many or as few masterpieces published as ever, but they will enter the world through proliferating channels. But for publishers, ordinary writers and booksellers, the next few years could be the last great days of publishing as we have known it since the last century.
>
> (Mundy, 2002: 31)

One thing is certain: constant change is here to stay – but many things will surely remain the same.

Reflections on the writing process

1   MOTIVATION: why do you write? What makes you decide to write an article/ a book chapter/a book/something in another category? What are the intrinsic and extrinsic factors here?

2   PLANNING, THINKING AND WRITING: how do the activities of planning, structuring and thinking occur during the writing process? For example, do you pre-plan or do it as you go along? Do you try to do most of your thinking before you start writing or do it as you go? How do you structure your writing, if at all?

3   THE WRITING PROCESS: do you try to write from 'beginning to end' or write sections at a time (out of sequence) and piece them together? Do you produce several drafts? Do you compose using pen and paper, or at the keyboard?

4   COLLABORATIVE WRITING: do you write with others? What do you see as the benefits of collaborative writing? Are there problems with it? *How* do you write with another or others? For example, do you ever actually compose with someone, e.g. together at the keyboard? Or do you write separately then piece things together?

5   GETTING FEEDBACK: do you ask a friend/colleague to comment on your writing? How do you choose this person? What do you look for from them? How do you feel about comments and feedback, including referees' comments?

6   ATTITUDE TO WRITING: do you enjoy it? What do you like *most* about it? And *least*? Is it a struggle or a pleasure or something else?

7   AIDS AND BARRIERS: do you find aids useful when writing, e.g. music, silence, your favourite desk, coffee . . . ? Do you get writer's block? How do you deal with it? Which times of the day (if any) suit you best for writing?

8   OTHER WRITING: do you write other things, e.g. poetry, newspaper articles and fiction? If so, how does this differ from academic writing? Does it help your academic writing in any way?

9   OPEN FORUM: is there anything else you would like to say about how you write, why, or any other aspect of writing?

Appendix 2

Interviews with journal editors

1 GENERAL INFORMATION AND BACKGROUND

What is the circulation of the journal? Who subscribes?

Who reads it, i.e. what categories of reader are there? Is it 'professional' or 'academic' or neither?

How long has it been established?

What is the rejection rate (if known)?

What sections does the journal have, e.g. reviews/letters/'position papers'/ research reports?

Do you have any documentation produced by the journal, e.g. notes for authors, policy statement, guidance or criteria forms for referees which can be shown?

Do you maintain any statistics on contributors over time, e.g. male/female split, status, occupation or position?

Is there a 'pecking order' amongst journals? If so, on what criteria is it based? Where is yours in the order?

2 THE EDITOR'S ROLE

How did you become editor?

What do you see as the role of the editor, e.g. in preliminary filtering, in selecting the editorial board . . .?

The editor and referees: what is the editor's role when referees disagree? Do you ever overrule referees? Do you check that modifications have been made?

Do you ever offer advice or guidance to potential authors, e.g. those who write letters of inquiry?

3 THE REFEREEING PROCESS

How do you (as editor) match submissions to referees?

Anonymity: do referees know who authors are? Do authors know who referees are?

What criteria do referees employ, explicitly and implicitly (if you have a feel for this)?

What do you see as the purpose of the peer-review process? Why do we do it?

4 USE OF THE EDITORIAL BOARD
How are members of the board selected?
What is the role of the board?

– Do they help shape policy and the journal's future?
– Do they meet to discuss issues?
– Do they help with difficult decisions or complaints made?
– Or do they act simply as referees?

5 IMPLICIT CRITERIA AND TACIT KNOWLEDGE
What do you really look for in a piece for your journal?

– What counts as a 'really good article'?
– What counts as a 'really bad one'?
What common complaints about submissions or common reasons for rejection
of submissions do you encounter?

6 GOING ELECTRONIC
Is there an e-version of the journal? Are there plans for one? Are there plans to
abandon the print-on-paper version?
Do you have a journal website? If so, what is it for? How is it used?
How are submissions handled, e.g. two hard copies, e-mail attachment?
Could you handle everything electronically up to production stage? Would you
want to? Would referees want you to?

7 OPEN FORUM
Is there anything else you would like to add about the journal, editing, the peer-
review process or journal publishing? Do you enjoy the job? What metaphor
would you use to describe your role, e.g. gatekeeper, disseminator, enhancer?

References

Agger, B. (1991). *A Critical Theory of Public Life*. London: Falmer Press.

Apple, M. (1999). 'What counts as legitimate knowledge? The social production and use of reviews.' *Review of Educational Research*, 69(4), 343–346.

Ashton-Jones, E. (1997). 'Co-authoring for scholarly publication: should you collaborate?' In: J. Moxley and T. Taylor (Eds), *Writing and Publishing for Academic Authors* (pp. 175–191). Lanham, USA: Rowman and Littlefield.

Bakanic, V., McPhail, C. and Simon, R. (1987). 'The manuscript review and decision-making process.' *American Sociological Review*, 52(October), 631–642.

Bandura, A. (1997). *Self-efficacy: the exercise of control*. New York: Freeman.

Bazerman, C. (1983). 'Scientific writing as a social act.' In: P. Anderson, J. Brockman and C. Miller (Eds), *New Essays in Technical Writing and Communication* (pp. 156–184). New York: Baywood.

Becker, H. (1986). *Writing for Social Scientists: how to start and finish your thesis, book or article*. Chicago: University of Chicago Press.

Bernard, A. (1990). *Rotten Rejections: a literary companion*. Wainscott, NY: Pushcart Press.

Bett, W. R. (1952). *The Preparation and Writing of Medical Papers for Publication*. London: Menley and James.

Boice, R. (1997). 'Strategies for enhancing scholarly productivity.' In: J. Moxley and T. Taylor (Eds), *Writing and Publishing for Academic Authors* (pp. 19–34). Lanham, USA: Rowman and Littlefield.

Bornstein, R. F. (1993). 'Costs and benefits of reviewer anonymity: a survey of journal editors and manuscript reviewers.' *Journal of Social Behaviour and Personality*, 8(3), 355–370.

Bourdieu, P. (1977). *Outline of a Theory of Practice*. (Translated by Richard Nise). New York: Cambridge University Press.

Bourdieu, P. (1998). *On Television and Journalism* (trans.). London: Pluto Press.

Brande, D. (1983). *Becoming a Writer*. London: Macmillan.

Brewer, B., Scherzer, C., Van Raalte, J. and Petipas, A. (2001). 'The elements of style: a survey of journal editors.' *American Psychologist*, 56(3), 266–267.

Bridges, D. (1999). 'Writing a research paper: reflections on a reflective log.' *Educational Action Research*, 7(2), 221–234.

Brookfield, S. (1995). *Becoming a Critically Reflective Teacher*. San Francisco: Jossey Bass.

Bush, V. (1945). 'As we may think.' *Atlantic Monthly*, 176(1), 101–108.

Close, F. (1991). *Too Hot to Handle: the race for cold fusion*. Princeton: Princeton University Press.

Davies, C. and Birbili, M. (2000). 'What do people need to know about writing in order to write in their jobs?' *British Journal of Educational Studies, 48*(4), 429–445.

Day, A. (1996). *How to Get Research Published in Journals*. Aldershot: Gower Press.

Deats, S. (1997). 'From podium to print: editing conference papers and publishing the dissertation.' In: J. Moxley and T. Taylor (Eds), *Writing and Publishing for Academic Authors* (pp. 127–140). Lanham, USA: Rowman and Littlefield.

Delton, J. (1985). *The 29 Most Common Writing Mistakes and How to Avoid Them*. Cincinnati: Writer's Digest Books.

Dies, R. (1993). 'Writing for publication.' *International Journal of Group Psychotherapy, 43*(2), 243–249.

Eagleton, T. (1983). *Literary Theory: an introduction*. Oxford: Blackwell.

Edwards, J. (1994). *The Scars of Dyslexia*. London: Cassell.

Eggleston, J. and Klein, G. (1997). *Achieving Publication in Education*. Stoke-on-Trent: Trentham Books.

Eisenhart, M. (2002). 'The paradox of peer review: admitting too much or allowing too little?' *Research in Science Education, 32*(2), 241–256.

Elbow, P. (1973). *Writing without Teachers*. Oxford: Oxford University Press.

Elbow, P. (1981). *Writing with Power*. Oxford: Oxford University Press.

Elton, L. (2000). 'The UK Research Assessment Exercise: unintended consequences.' *Higher Education Quarterly, 54*(3), 274–283.

Fiske, D. and Fogg, L. (1990). 'But the reviewers are making different criticisms of my paper! Diversity and uniqueness in reviewer comments.' *American Psychologist, 45*, 591–598.

Flower, L. and Hayes, J. (1981). 'The pregnant pause: an inquiry into the nature of planning.' *Research in the Teaching of English, 15*, 229–243.

Foucault, M. (1980). *Power/Knowledge: selected interviews and other writings 1972–1977*. London: Harvester Wheatsheaf.

Glass, G. (1999). 'A new day in how scholars communicate.' *Current Issues in Education, 2*(2), 1–4.

Grabe, W. and Kaplan, R. (1996). *Theory and Practice of Writing*. New York: Longman.

Hargreaves, D. (1996). *Teaching as a Research-based Profession: possibilities and prospects*. London: Teacher Training Agency (TTA).

Hartley, J. (1992a). 'Writing: a review of the research.' In: J. Hartley (Ed.), *Technology and Writing: readings in the psychology of written communication* (pp. 18–36). London: Jessica Kingsley.

Hartley, J. (Ed.) (1992b). *Technology and Writing: readings in the psychology of written communication*. London: Jessica Kingsley.

Hartley, J. (1997). 'Writing the thesis.' In: N. Graves and V. Varma (Eds), *Working for a Doctorate* (pp. 96–112). London: Routledge.

Hartley, J. and Branthwaite, A. (1989). 'The psychologist as wordsmith: a questionnaire study of the writing strategies of productive British psychologists.' *Higher Education, 18*, 423–452.

Hartley, J. and Knapper, C. (1984). 'Academics and their writing.' *Studies in Higher Education, 9*, 151–167.

Hayes, J. and Flower, L. (1986). 'Writing research and the writer.' *American Psychologist*, *41*(10), 1106–1113.

Haynes, A. (2001). *Writing Successful Textbooks*. London: A & C Black.

Henson, K. (1999). *Writing for Professional Publication*. Boston: Allyn and Bacon.

Hillage, J., Pearson, R., Anderson, A. and Tamkin, P. (1998). *Excellence in Research on Schools*. London: DFEE.

Hills, P. J. (Ed.) (1987). *Publish or Perish*. Ely, Cambridgeshire: Peter Francis.

Holmes, O. (1974). 'Thesis to book: what to get rid of.' *Scholarly Publishing* 5, 339–349.

Holmes, O. (1975). 'Thesis to book: what to do with what is left.' *Scholarly Publishing* 7, 166–176.

Humes, A. (1983). 'Research on the composing process.' *Review of Educational Research*, *53*(2), 201–216.

Jones, S. (1996). *In the Blood*. London: HarperCollins.

Lakoff, G. and Johnson, M. (1980). *Metaphors We Live By*. Chicago: University of Chicago Press.

Larochelle, M. and Desautels, J. (2002). 'On peers, those particular friends.' *Research in Science Education*, *32*(2), 181–189.

Lather, P. (1999). 'To be of use: the work of reviewing.' *Review of Educational Research*, *69*(1), 2–7.

Mahoney, M., Kazdin, A. and Kenigsberg, M. (1978). 'Getting published.' *Cognitive Therapy and Research*, *2*(1), 69–70.

McCallum, C. (1997). *Writing for Publication* (fourth edn). Oxford: How to Books Ltd.

Medawar, P. (1963). 'Is the scientific paper a fraud?' *The Listener*, September.

Medawar, P. (1979). *Advice to a Young Scientist*. New York: Harper and Row.

Merton, R. (1968). 'The Matthew effect in science.' *Science*, *159*, 56–63.

Midgley, S. (2002). 'The end of books?' *Guardian*, 9 April, 15.

Moxley, J. (1997). 'If not now, when?' In: J. Moxley and T. Taylor (Eds), *Writing and Publishing for Academic Authors* (pp. 6–19). Lanham, USA: Rowman and Littlefield.

Moxley, J. and Taylor, T. (Eds) (1997). *Writing and Publishing for Academic Authors* (second edn). Lanham, USA: Rowman and Littlefield.

Mullen, C. (2001). 'The need for a curricular writing model for graduate students.' *Journal of Further and Higher Education*, *25*(1), 117–126.

Mundy, T. (2002). 'Good books.' *Prospect*, October, 24–31.

Nixon, J. (1999). 'Teachers, writers, professionals. Is there anybody out there?' *British Journal of Sociology of Education*, *20*(2), 207–221.

Noble, K. (1989). 'Publish or perish: what 23 journal editors have to say.' *Studies in Higher Education*, *14*(1), 97–102.

Osborne, M. and Brady, D. (2002). 'The room is long and narrow.' *Research in Science Education*, *32*(2), 163–169.

Packwood, A., Scanlon, M. and Weiner, G. (1997). *Getting Published: a study of writing, refereeing and editing practices*. Swindon: Economic and Social Science Research Council.

Peters, D. and Ceci, S. (1982). 'Peer review practices of psychological journals: the fate of published articles, submitted again.' *The Behavioural and Brain Sciences*, *5*, 187–255.

Phillips, E. and Pugh, D. (1994). *How to Get a Ph.D.* (second edn). Buckingham: Open University Press.

Popkewitz, T. and Brennan, M. (1998). *Foucault's Challenge*. New York: Teachers College Press.

Powell, W. (1985). *Getting into Print: the decision making process in scholarly publishing*. Chicago: University of Chicago Press.

Quiller-Couch, A. (1916). *On the Art of Writing*. London: Putnam.

Richardson, L. (1985). *The New Other Woman: contemporary single women in affairs with married men*. New York: Free Press.

Richardson, L. (1987). 'Disseminating research to popular audiences: the book tour.' *Qualitative Sociology*, 19(2), 164–176.

Richardson, L. (1990). *Writing Strategies: reaching diverse audiences*. Newbury Park: Sage.

Richardson, L. (1998). 'Writing: a method of inquiry.' In: N. Denzin and Y. Lincoln (Eds), *Collecting and Interpreting Qualitative Materials*. London: Sage.

Roth, M. (2002). 'Editorial power/authorial suffering.' *Research in Science Education*, 32(2), 215–240.

Scardamalia, M. and Bereiter, C. (1987). 'Knowledge telling and knowledge transforming in written composition.' In: S. Rosenberg (Ed.), *Reading, Writing and Language Learning*. Cambridge: Cambridge University Press.

Smaby, H., Crews, J. and Downing, T. (1999). 'Publishing in scholarly journals: part II – is it an attitude or a technique? It's an attitude.' *Counselor Education and Supervision*, 38(June), 227–236.

Smedley, C. (1993). *Getting Your Book Published*. California: Sage.

Smith, B. and Gough, P. (1984). 'Editors speak out on refereeing.' *Phi Delta Kappa*, May, 637–639.

Sobel, D. (1996). *Longitude*. London: Fourth Estate.

Sprent, P. (1995). *Getting into Print*. London: E & F N Spon.

Sternberg, R. (2002). *On Civility in Reviewing* [Internet source]. Retrieved, 2002, from the World Wide Web: http://www.psychologicalscience.org/observer/0102/prescol.html

Talib, A. (2000). 'The RAE and publications: a review of journal editors.' *Higher Education Review*, 33(No.1), 1–5.

Thomas, G. (1987). 'The process of writing a scientific paper.' In: P. J. Hills (Ed.), *Publish or Perish* (pp. 93–117). Ely, Cambridgeshire: Peter Francis.

Thyer, B. (1994). *Successful Publishing in Scholarly Journals*. Thousand Oaks, California: Sage.

Tobin, K. (2002). 'The multiple faces of peer review in science education.' *Research in Science Education*, 32(2), 135–156.

Tooley, J. and Darby, D. (1998). *Educational Research: a critique*. London: Office for Standards in Education (OFSTED).

Underwood, B. (1957). *Psychological Research*. New York: Appleton-Century-Crofts.

Wason, P. C. (1980). 'Specific thoughts on the writing process.' In: L. Gregg and E. Steinberg (Eds), *Cognitive Processes in Writing* (pp. 129–137). Hillsdale, New Jersey: Erlbaum.

Weiner, G. (2001). 'The academic journal: has it a future?' *Education Policy Analysis Archives (EPAA, available on-line)*, 9(9), 1–18.

Wellington, J. (1989). *Education for Employment*. Windsor: NFER-Nelson.

Wellington, J. (2000). *Educational Research: contemporary issues and practical approaches*. London and New York: Continuum.

Williams, J. (1987). 'Covert linguistic behaviour during writing tasks.' *Written Communication*, 4, 310–328.

Willinsky, J. (2000). 'Proposing a knowledge exchange model for scholarly publishing.' *Current Issues in Education*, 3(6), 1–26.

Wolcott, H. (1990). *Writing Up Qualitative Research*. Newbury Park: Sage.

Woodhead, C. (1997, 21 January). *Inspecting Schools: the key to raising standards*. Paper presented at the Royal Geographic Society, London.

Woodhead, N. (1991). *Hypertext and Hypermedia: theory and applications*. Wilmslow: Sigma Press/Addison-Wesley.

Woods, P. (1999). *Successful Writing for Qualitative Researchers*. London: Routledge.

Woodwark, J. (1992). *How to Run a Paper Mill: writing technical papers and getting them published*. Winchester: Information Geometers Ltd.

Zinsser, W. (1983). *Writing with a Word Processor*. New York: Harper and Row.

Zuckerman, H. (1970). 'Stratification in American science.' *Sociological Inquiry*, 40(2), 235–257.

Zuckerman, H. and Merton, R. (1971). 'Patterns of evaluation in science.' *Minerva*, 9, 66–100.

Index